SUMMERTIME

(Il Paese delle Vacanze)

An Idyll in Three Acts

by

UGO BETTI

Translated by

HENRY REED

LONDON

SAMUEL FRENCH LIMITED

SUMMERTIME

Produced at the Apollo Theatre, London, on the 9th November 1955, with the following cast of characters—

(in the order of their appearance)

CLEOFE	*Gwen Ffrangcon Davies*
FRANCESCA, her niece	*Geraldine McEwan*
OFELIA, a neighbour	*Esma Cannon*
ADELAIDE, Cleofe's maid	*Maureen Quinney*
ALBERTO, Ofelia's nephew	*Dirk Bogarde*
THE POSTMAN	*Tony Church*
*A COMMERCIAL TRAVELLER	—
NOEMI	*Vivienne Drummond*
THE DOCTOR	*Michael Gwynn*
CONSALVO, Noemi's brother	*Mark Dignam*
A FARMER	*Ronald Barker*
*MARIA	*Barbara New*

Produced by PETER HALL
Settings by JAMES BAILEY

SYNOPSIS OF SCENES

ACT I

Two small neighbouring cottage gardens. A Summer morning

ACT II

An Alpine spot not far from the Madonna of the Mountain.
A little over an hour later

ACT III

A room in the house of a local peasant. A few hours later

Time—the present

* Some alterations have been made to the sets in this play. The Acting Edition does not therefore correspond in all respects with the Apollo Theatre production. The character MARIA has been dropped in this edition of the play and the COMMERCIAL TRAVELLER has been added.

The fee for one performance of this play by amateurs is Five Guineas, payable in advance to us, or to our authorized agents.

The performance of this play by amateurs may be restricted in certain territories overseas, and amateurs intending production outside the British Isles must make application to us, or to our authorized agents, before starting rehearsals or booking a theatre or hall.

Upon payment of the fee a licence will be issued for the performance to take place. No performance may be given unless this licence has first been obtained.

In the event of further performances being given, the fee for each and every performance subsequent to the first is Four Guineas. This reduction applies only in the case of the performances being **consecutive** and at the **same theatre or hall.**

The following particulars are needed for the issue of a licence:

Title of the play
Name of the town
Name of the theatre or hall
Date of the performance(s)
Name and address of the applicant
Name of the society

Please state the amount remitted with the application.

Character costumes and wigs used in the performance of plays contained in French's Acting Edition may be obtained from Messrs CHARLES H. FOX LTD, 184 High Holborn, London, W.C.1

SUMMERTIME

ACT I

Scene—*Two small neighbouring cottage gardens. A Summer morning·
  The gardens are separated by a varnished wooden fence which is low
enough to be stepped over. This commences down R and runs in a curve
up RC. The cottages themselves are not visible, though one can see the
door of a hen-house among the bushes down L. The garden walls run
across the back. Behind these the high road can be seen. The garden L is
that of Miss Cleofe and the garden R that of Miss Ofelia. Miss Cleofe's
garden gate is RC of the wall and leads on to the road. The gate of the
other garden is not seen. On the far side of the road are trees and bushes
with a wide expanse of sky beyond. Down L is a garden table with
basket chairs above and R of it. Against the fence down R is a low bench.
Above the bench is a dwarf apple tree.*
  (*See the Ground Plan at the end of the Play*)

When the Curtain *rises,* Francesca *is seated above the table, quietly
preparing and wrapping sandwiches.* Cleofe *is prowling about her
garden. The song of a number of caged canaries can be heard.* Cleofe,
armed with spectacles, moves to the apple tree and counts the apples.

Cleofe (*counting*) One. Two. Three. Four. Five. (*She counts
again*) . . . Three. Four. *Five.* (*Indignantly*) I would just like to know
who's had the sixth, that's all. It was here on this very tree last
night.

Francesca. Perhaps it was the milk boy, Aunt.

Cleofe (*who rarely pauses for breath*) Perhaps it was; I've never
liked that boy. But it wouldn't surprise *me* very much if someone
else had taken a fancy to it. It's not the apple I mind about,
though of course it had to be the very best one on the tree. It's the
principle of the thing. You might *think*, considering what close
friends we've been all these years, in and out of each other's
houses all day long, *you might think* he'd have the common decency
to *ask* for the apple. Do you know what I'd have done? I'd have
picked all six of them for him. Not just the one, all six: and I'd
have sent them round to him, done up properly, in a nice little
basket. Wouldn't I?

Francesca. Yes, Aunt Cleofe, you would.

Cleofe (*unwearied*) Or we could have taken them with us on
the picnic today, and eaten them up there, all together. Friend-
ship is one thing, fruit's another. But no. Every time the great
Alberto comes here, you find there's an apple missing. It would
be just the same if he had measles. When there aren't any apples,

it's plums. (*She crosses towards Francesca*) Did you hear him last night? He can't even get home at a respectable hour now. And as thin as a rake. And it isn't just work in the city that makes him so thin. (*She sits* R *of the table*) Did you hear him last night?

FRANCESCA. Yes, Aunt.

CLEOFE. I should just think so, he'd have woken a man in a trance. I don't know why anyone should have to make a row like that at night, when decent people are in bed asleep. (*She looks satirically over her shoulder in the direction of the neighbouring garden* R) And now, of course, *he's* asleep; and leaving us to do the work. He kindly condescends to come on the picnic with us; but who has to do the sandwiches? We do. What do you think he'd say if *I* started to whistle about the place, and race about the garden, and bang all the heavy furniture about in the middle of the night? I still can't think what he was doing. There was something very odd going on.

FRANCESCA. Perhaps he was just feeling happy, Aunt Cleofe.

CLEOFE. Well, I'm happy, too, sometimes. You never hear me whistle, do you? And there's another thing I don't approve of. (*Intensely*) How can he *lower* himself to a stride over the fence? What's the garden gate there for?

FRANCESCA. He does it because it's quicker.

CLEOFE. I dare say. But it's the principle of the thing. It's rude; it's slovenly. In my day I'm glad to think we had a little more style. (*She rises restlessly, moves* C *and contemplates the other garden* R) I suppose he thinks now they've offered him all these fine jobs in the city, he's above our poor little garden gate. In any case, I don't believe in all these jobs they keep talking about. They've been asking for him, and waiting for him, and I don't know what, for the last two months. Well, he can go as soon as he likes for all I care. He can go tomorrow, if he wants to. (*She turns to Francesca*) Did you say something?

FRANCESCA. No, Aunt.

CLEOFE (*moving to* R *of the table*) Are you sorry he's going?

FRANCESCA. But, Aunt, they only said he *might* be going.

CLEOFE. His aunt talks of nothing else, all day long: Alberto's splendid new job. Oh, she's not a bad woman, I'm not saying she is. But she never stops talking. She's a know-all. As well anyone might be who spends the whole day behind the shutters peering into what's going on in other people's houses through her late brother's *celebrated marine binoculars*. Not a very dignified thing to do, I would have thought.

(*Tapping sounds are heard off* R)

FRANCESCA (*warningly*) Shhh!

CLEOFE. What's the matter.

FRANCESCA (*nodding towards the other garden*) How very odd. I can hear tapping.

CLEOFE (*crossing almost to the fence* RC) Good heavens, you'd think they were knocking nails in.

FRANCESCA (*rising and following Cleofe*) There's someone in Alberto's room.

CLEOFE. Well, what did I tell you. Showing off. We're down here getting the picnic things ready, we leave in half an hour, and they can't even nod to us from the window. Your great Alberto ...

(FRANCESCA *returns to the table, resumes her seat and arranges the things on it, so that they may be packed up*)

FRANCESCA. Oh, but he'll be here presently, Aunt.

CLEOFE. I know he will. The minute he smells my tarts he'll be out like a shot, you can be sure of that.

FRANCESCA. But his aunt will have made some tarts, too, Aunt.

CLEOFE (*moving up* C) There are tarts and tarts, my dear Francesca. The fact remains that every year we go on this wonderful picnic; we take our tarts, they take their tarts; which tarts come back? Theirs. There must be some reason for it, I suppose. Never so much as a *flake* of mine do you see brought back. (*She looks off* L *and calls elaborately*) Adelaide. Isn't it about time you were taking the tartlets out of the oven?

ADELAIDE (*off* L; *calling*) I'm just taking them out, Miss Cleofe.

CLEOFE (*loudly*) And don't forget to grease them well, will you?

ADELAIDE (*off*) I'm just greasing them now, Miss Cleofe.

CLEOFE. Thank you. (*She moves down* C) The truth of the matter *is*: your precious Alberto eats more of my tarts than all the rest of us put together. It surprises me he never gets stomach ache. It makes you think the meals he gets in the city must be barely enough to keep him going, in spite of all these wonderful *posts*. Do you know what *I* think, Francesca? I don't believe all this nonsense about big jobs in the city. I've seen too many people end up in the gutter. Even in jail sometimes.

FRANCESCA. Oh, do let's hope not, Aunt Cleofe.

CLEOFE. Let's hope not. But you know what happens in these big cities: bad companions, bad habits—and—(*she lowers her voice and moves to Francesca*) women. Alberto is the sort of lad who's *designed* for trouble, you can see it in his face. Would you call Alberto a *bright* young man?

FRANCESCA. Well—not altogether perhaps.

CLEOFE (*sitting* R *of the table*) I have no wish to compare him with the doctor. I'm not speaking of his education, of course. That's not his fault, it's the way they're taught nowadays. But, if you ask me, the trouble is Fibre. That's what it all comes down to Fibre. Alberto's a good boy, no doubt, but he has no Fibre. You wouldn't say there's anything very splendid or remarkable about Alberto, would you?

Francesca. Oh, no, he's just a good, nice boy, that's all.

Cleofe. Ah! In my day a man was expected to appeal to a woman's imagination. A woman's heart. We insisted on it. A man had to *have* something. He even had to be—a bit of a scamp. (*Reminiscently*) My word, yes.

Francesca. I don't think there's anything unpleasant about Alberto.

Cleofe. No, you can't even say that for him. He isn't clever, he isn't handsome, he isn't rich, he has no Fibre. And we can't even pretend he's unpleasant.

Francesca (*without raising her eyes*) But, Auntie, you've said yourself . . .

Cleofe. Yes, yes, I like him, I know. I'm not made of flint. I've seen him grow up. He's a good lad. (*She notices something unusual going on next door, breaks off, rises, moves up* c *and stares in silence for a few moments along the road to* r) That's very strange.

Francesca (*rising*) What is, Aunt?

Cleofe. Their maid's just gone out. I could have sworn she'd got letters to post. I saw them in her hand. And they're still knocking those nails in.

Francesca. I wonder what's the matter.

Cleofe. Well, what should be the matter? They're just very important people, that's all. And, in the meantime, *we* have to get on with cutting up sandwiches. (*She looks off* l *and calls*) Adelaide. How have those tartlets turned out? Have they risen?

Adelaide (*off* l; *calling*) Most of them, Miss Cleofe. Most of them have.

Cleofe. As soon as you've greased them, bring them out here with some wrapping-up paper, will you?

Adelaide (*off*) Yes, Miss Cleofe.

Cleofe (*moving to Francesca; with a change of tone*) Francesca.

Francesca. Yes, Aunt?

Cleofe. You look very nice in that jacket.

Francesca. I put it on for the picnic.

Cleofe. You've grown into a fine girl, Francesca. It seems only yesterday you were in pinafores. (*She pauses and gently pushes Francesca into her seat, then sits* r *of the table*) I think it's about time you were thinking of getting married, Francesca.

Francesca. *I've* no objection, Aunt.

Cleofe. All your friends are getting engaged and married. (*She lowers her voice a little*) Francesca, last night after you'd gone out the doctor was talking to me again. Oh, nothing unusual; but you wouldn't have to be a mind reader to see that he'd be very glad to marry you. He's a man with very fine qualities, the doctor.

Francesca. Don't you think he's rather a bore?

Cleofe. So a husband should be. When husbands are entertaining, you very soon find it's not their wives they entertain.

It's other women. The doctor's a fine figure of a man. Nice voice. Manly. Well-bred. Got on very well in his profession. And quite well off. A woman would find him a great comfort about the place.

FRANCESCA. I don't like the way the doctor does his hair.

CLEOFE (*rising indignantly*) Francesca, you're not a child any longer. The doctor's just the sort of man who makes a woman really happy. His brother, the one who married Giovanna Rossi, takes her up a pot of coffee and two boiled eggs in bed every morning. I know it for a fact. That's what I call a husband. A man who runs and gets something to put round his wife's shoulders the minute it begins to get chilly.

FRANCESCA. But, Aunt, if I were married, *I* should be the one who wanted to take my husband *his* breakfast in bed, and put something round his shoulders when it got chilly.

CLEOFE. My dear Francesca, I've got a horrible fear you're the kind of girl who's fated to get herself made a *victim* of. (*She turns and moves a few paces* C)

FRANCESCA. Oh, I hope not, Aunt Cleofe.

CLEOFE (*turning*) Francesca.

FRANCESCA. Yes, Aunt?

CLEOFE. Everyone knows you're in love with Alberto. A blind man could see it.

FRANCESCA (*calmly; as though it were unimportant*) I like him.

CLEOFE. Head over heels, I should have said. More's the pity. And what are you going to do about it, may I ask?

FRANCESCA (*as before*) I'd like to marry him.

CLEOFE. Oh. Well, you seem fairly clear on the point. What about him, what does he say?

FRANCESCA. Nothing.

CLEOFE. What do you mean: nothing?

FRANCESCA (*calmly*) I don't think he's noticed.

CLEOFE (*staggered*) Alberto's *never noticed* you're madly in love with him?

FRANCESCA. I don't think so, Aunt.

CLEOFE. Are you sure he's not pretending? Men are very crafty.

FRANCESCA. No, I really don't think so.

CLEOFE. God bless my soul! (*She gives a look of indignant contempt towards the next garden*) What a—*turnip!* Young men were very different in my day. They were—full of ardour. But, my dear child, haven't you tried—in any way—(*she moves to Francesca*) to *show* him what you feel?

FRANCESCA. Well, you can imagine, Aunt.

CLEOFE. Yes, I can imagine. Perfectly well. I only asked as a formality. And Alberto still . . .

FRANCESCA. Nothing.

CLEOFE (*indignantly*) And what do you intend to do about it?

FRANCESCA (*wrapping the sandwiches in a napkin; calmly*) I intend to marry him, Aunt.

CLEOFE. But doesn't it make your blood boil to think he never notices you?

FRANCESCA (*calmly*) I could punch his head.

CLEOFE. When there are lots of young men who are falling over each other just to look at you.

FRANCESCA. It's because we've grown up together, you see, Aunt. He still thinks I'm just a boy friend, in spite of my skirts.

CLEOFE. Boy friend! Doesn't he ever wonder why you haven't done your military service? (*She sits* R *of the table*)

FRANCESCA. A boy friend, that's how he sees me. It can't be helped.

CLEOFE. And how is it you don't think of him as a girl friend in trousers?

FRANCESCA (*resigned*) I think it must all have begun when I was very little. Whenever I used to play at being a lady I had to have a gentleman, and as there were no other boys except Alberto about the place, it always had to be Alberto.

CLEOFE. Is that how it was?

FRANCESCA. Yes, that was it. (*Wistfully*) Aunt, do you remember when poor Uncle Venturino had gallstones, and he said it used to give him a terrible pain right deep down? Well, that's how I feel whenever I think of Alberto marrying anyone else.

CLEOFE (*after a pause*) Your uncle always exaggerated everything, of course. Francesca, my dear, *I* wasn't such a bad-looking girl, when I was young. *I also* used to go with young gentlemen on picnics up in the mountains just like we do now. And look at me. I'm just an old parrot now, that's all. Time races on, Francesca. You mustn't let it slip past you like this.

FRANCESCA. But I don't want it to slip past, Auntie.

CLEOFE. I'm quite sure if I'd been in your place, I'd have seen to it that—some little thing or other happened, to make him *do* something. Oh, something quite innocent, I mean, of course.

FRANCESCA (*in a low voice*) I do think up things, sometimes. For example, I sometimes imagine . . . You won't laugh at me, will you?

CLEOFE. I may even envy you, my dear.

FRANCESCA. I imagine that I've had some great sorrow or other. For example, a death in the family, perhaps . . .

CLEOFE. Let's hope there'll still be time for that.

FRANCESCA. A death in the family—and I'm standing there crying, just by the apple tree. And suddenly Alberto comes out . . .

CLEOFE (*resignedly*) Striding over the fence, no doubt.

FRANCESCA. And he comes up to me to comfort me. And then I throw myself sobbing on his chest.

CLEOFE (*doubtfully*) Yes, well, he *might* give you a little squeeze, I dare say. That wouldn't get you very far.

FRANCESCA (*shyly*) Once something did happen rather like that. I'd been frightened. By a lizard.

CLEOFE (*curious rather than severe*) And you actually threw yourself on his chest?

FRANCESCA. Yes.

CLEOFE. What did he do?

FRANCESCA (*with a gesture*) He put his hand here.

CLEOFE (*interested*) On his heart?

FRANCESCA. No, on his fountain pen. He was afraid I'd broken it.

CLEOFE. Bah! (*Sympathetically*) My poor Francesca—I shouldn't be a woman if I didn't understand. (*She rises in sudden surprise and looks off* R) Good gracious! What on earth are they doing with rope?

FRANCESCA. Rope? (*She rises*)

CLEOFE. Their maid has just gone in again with a coil of rope.

FRANCESCA. And they haven't even watered the flowers this morning.

CLEOFE. There's something going on. (*She crosses to the fence*) I can sense it. (*She raises her voice and evidently greets her neighbour*) Good morning, Miss Ofelia.

OFELIA (*off* R; *as from an upper window, in busy tones*) Good morning, good morning.

(FRANCESCA *crosses to Cleofe*)

Have you heard? Wonderful news! Great news for Alberto. I'll be with you in a jiffy.

(*There is a pause. Evidently* OFELIA *has withdrawn from the window.* FRANCESCA, *shaken by Ofelia's words, sits suddenly on the bench down* R, *her back to the next door garden*)

CLEOFE (*moving to Francesca*) Now, there's nothing to worry about, Francesca. My dear child, you've gone quite pale. "Good news for Alberto." Such nonsense! Never you mind, my dear. (*She sits beside Francesca, pauses, then speaks in a new, resolute, almost masculine tone*) Francesca.

FRANCESCA. Yes, Aunt?

CLEOFE. Officially, Francesca, I ought to be against all this. But, privately speaking, I'm dying to help you. We must make up our minds at once.

FRANCESCA. About what, Aunt?

CLEOFE. We must act. There's no time to lose. He may be leaving any minute. The world is full of shameless women. They'll snap him up and marry him, and all you'll get is the news.

FRANCESCA. What do you think I ought to do?

CLEOFE. Bring him to the point. Today. Up there. At the

picnic. It may be only a matter of hours, Francesca. Why don't you try and make him jealous of the doctor? While we're all up there? Or better still: sprain your ankle. It's quite usual. It's often done. He'll be forced to pick you up and carry you. And after that the—well, the rest will be up to you.

FRANCESCA (*doubtfully*) But, Aunt, you see that sort of thing the whole time at the pictures. (*She drops her eyes*) And in any case, Aunt Cleofe, I—I've thought of something else. (*She rises, moves up* C *and stands with her back to Cleofe*) Another way.

CLEOFE. You've thought of one already?

FRANCESCA. Yes.

CLEOFE. What way?

FRANCESCA (*turning to face Cleofe; calmly*) I shall tell him.

CLEOFE. Tell him?

FRANCESCA. Yes.

CLEOFE (*alarmed*) Tell him what?

FRANCESCA. Everything.

CLEOFE (*after a pause; more alarmed*) What, straight out? Today?

FRANCESCA. Yes, Aunt.

CLEOFE. You'll propose to him—yourself?

FRANCESCA. I think—it's probably safer that way.

(CLEOFE *rises*)

CLEOFE (*after a pause; with admiration*) Francesca, if I'd been a man, I'd like to have married you myself.

(MISS OFELIA *enters* R. *She is aged fifty.* CLEOFE *and* FRANCESCA *turn to face her*)

OFELIA. Good morning, everybody. Good morning.

CLEOFE
FRANCESCA} (*together*) Good morning.

OFELIA (*importantly*) Girls, I'm covered with dust. Literally.

CLEOFE (*crossing to the table and inspecting the sandwiches; indifferently*) Anything happened?

OFELIA (*triumphantly*) Happened! He's leaving.

CLEOFE. Leaving? Who is?

OFELIA. Alberto, of course. To take up his new post. They want him at once.

CLEOFE (*contemptuously*) Who does?

OFELIA (*rather piqued*) The bank.

CLEOFE (*aggressively*) Whatever for?

OFELIA. What for? Why, he's being given a confidential post.

CLEOFE. What's he going to do with it?

OFELIA. Well—he'll—*run* things.

CLEOFE (*sourly*) Run a bank? (*She puts her spectacles on the chair* R *of the table*)

OFELIA. I didn't say that. But they certainly want him for a very important post. (*She lowers her voice*) He'll have a room to himself.

CLEOFE (*a little taken aback*) We've been hearing about that room to himself for the last two months. When's he going?

OFELIA. Why, immediately, my dear. Today. Tomorrow. I don't know quite. You know what these banks are. Everything's a matter of urgency.

FRANCESCA (*a little unsteadily*) But—what about the picnic this afternoon? W-won't Alberto be able to come to the picnic?

OFELIA. Why, my dear, I can't say. I shouldn't think so. It's a big change in his life, this is, you know.

CLEOFE (*moving and standing near Francesca; very angry*) You mean, he's not coming to the picnic?

OFELIA. I'm afraid not. I'm so sorry.

CLEOFE. And you wait till *now* to come and tell us.

OFELIA. I'm sorry, my dear. I've been making tarts for it, too. But we've too much to do, girls. I'm sure you understand.

FRANCESCA (*faintly*) But—won't he even come to say good-bye to us? And talk to us a bit?

OFELIA. Well, he's terribly busy, poor boy. But, oh, of course, he'll come and say good-bye. Just for a minute last thing tonight.

CLEOFE (*after a pause*) Ah. Just for a minute. Last thing to-night. We'll see about that. (*She looks off* L *and calls solemnly*) Adelaide. Bring the tartlets out here.

ADELAIDE (*off*) I was just bringing them, Miss Cleofe.

(ADELAIDE, *Cleofe's maid, enters* L. *She carries a wooden dish laden with tarts*)

CLEOFE (*indicating the bench down* R) Just put them down over there; where they can be seen.

(ADELAIDE *crosses, puts the dish on the bench, then crosses and exits* L)

OFELIA. Oh, how lovely, how lovely. What a lovely, lovely smell. Clever Adelaide.

CLEOFE. Clever Francesca, you mean. She measured all the ingredients out herself. You don't find many girls like Francesca these days.

(ALBERTO *enters* R *and steps across the fence. He is aged twenty-eight. He is in his shirt-sleeves*)

ALBERTO (*as he enters*) Good morning, everyone. What a lovely smell.

CLEOFE (*dryly*) Good morning.

FRANCESCA (*moving slowly to the table*) Hello, Alberto.

ALBERTO. Hello. Have you all heard? The bank has sent for us at last. The main branch.

CLEOFE. Let's hope it doesn't snap off.

ALBERTO (*his eyes on the tarts*) No. We shall be there, Aunt
Cleofe. Eyes like a lynx and wrists of steel. (*He wanders to the bench,
picks up the dish of tarts and inspects them*)

CLEOFE. And plenty of lick—I trust.

ALBERTO. Lick?

CLEOFE. For sticking down envelopes.

OFELIA (*hurt*) Oh, but Alberto's going to have tremendous
great offices.

ALBERTO (*detaching a piece of crust from one of the tarts and eating it*)
Sorry, Aunt Cleofe, I was just taking a crumb off one of your
tarts. It was flaking off. The truth is, these wily old bankers know
what they're doing. (*He replaces the dish on the bench*)

OFELIA. They understand. They know how to appreciate the
right people.

(FRANCESCA *moves the chair* R *of the table and places it* C)

ALBERTO. Whoever would have thought that . . . Sorry, Aunt
Cleofe, I might as well have this little bit, mightn't I? It was
flaking off. Lovely. (*He crosses to* C) I was saying, whoever would
have thought they'd had their eyes on me all this time.

OFELIA. You're too modest, Alberto. That's your trouble.

(ALBERTO *sinks into the armchair* C. CLEOFE *moves* LC. FRAN-
CESCA *gets the dish of tarts and places them thoughtfully beside Alberto*)

ALBERTO. Auff! I've done nothing but strap up suitcases all
morning. I'm worn out. I'm all for the simple life myself. All these
important jobs—rushing around the whole time. I get fed up
with it, you know.

OFELIA. There. That's your modesty again.

ALBERTO (*detaching another piece of crust from the tarts*) I say,
Aunt Cleofe, these tarts really are marvellous. They melt in the
mouth.

CLEOFE. So it would seem. Help yourself.

(ALBERTO *takes a tart*)

And *I'm* not your aunt. That's your aunt.

ALBERTO (*with his mouth full*) Do you know what I've been
thinking? I've been thinking all morning about how I've got to
leave you, Aunt Cleofe and Francesca. And Aunt Ofelia, too, of
course, only she'll be joining me in the city later on. But when I
thought of it all, do you know, I felt something dreadful *here*? My
stomach seemed to close right up.

CLEOFE (*with a glance at him*) One would hardly have thought
so.

ALBERTO (*nostalgically*) What memories. What wonderful
years. It seems only yesterday we first came here for the holidays.
Do you remember, Aunt Cleofe, when I broke that branch? The
branch of the old pear tree.

CLEOFE. Yes. And poor little Francesca took all the blame herself, as usual, to get you out of it. And you let her be smacked for it.

OFELIA. Yes, but he was very young at the time.

CLEOFE. Well, wasn't Francesca? She was younger than he was. She always has been. And she let them smack her without a whimper. For *you*, Alberto. Ah, Francesca's got you out of a lot of trouble before now.

ALBERTO (*with his mouth full*) Wonderful times. I'll send you a new pear tree, Aunt Cleofe, shall I? From the city. A present. A Japanese pear tree. Have you ever seen one? It's a pear tree that looks like an apple tree. It has apple blossom, and it grows lovely apples on it. It's exactly like an apple tree. Only it's a pear. It's Japanese. And a watering can. I'll send you one of those with a pump. The sort you squirt.

CLEOFE (*suspiciously*) A watering can?

ALBERTO. Yes. Yours must have got a bit dented in. Last night. It got under my foot—and the fuchsias as well. I'll see to all that.

CLEOFE (*alarmed*) My fuchsias?

ALBERTO (*his mouth still full*) Yes. I told you: the watering can tripped me up. I think I must have landed up in the fuchsia bed. (*He breaks off, fumbles beneath himself and produces Cleofe's spectacles*) Oh, Aunt Cleofe, now that *is* your fault. You really shouldn't leave your glasses about the place like that.

CLEOFE (*taking the spectacles from Alberto; with resigned fury*) You've sat on my spectacles. You haven't broken anything else, I suppose, by any chance?

ALBERTO (*rising*) Come, come, Aunt Cleofe, don't be cross. (*Coaxing*) Forget and forgive, m'm? *Yes*. It may be a very long time before I break anything else of yours, after all. I'll send you a whole great pile of presents from the city. And to Francesca, too; I'll send cartloads of them. Shall I, Francesca? (*He resumes his seat*)

CLEOFE. "Shall I, Francesca?" Yes, we know. She'll soon get tired of looking out for *them*. Her big day has arrived, too. She'll be getting married very shortly.

ALBERTO. Francesca?

CLEOFE. Yes, Francesca. She's a lovely girl. Everyone says so. Of course, she'll be getting married.

ALBERTO (*not very pleased*) I—I don't see what that's got to do with anything. Surely, it's a bit premature, isn't it? Francesca's still—well, I mean, she's still—so undeveloped.

CLEOFE (*coldly*) Well, some we could name don't seem to think so.

OFELIA. Oh, Cleofe, *really*? Is that so? How lovely. Is there really something—brewing?

CLEOFE (*sharply*) Brewing?

OFELIA. Well—you know.

FRANCESCA (*embarrassed*) I wish there were. (*She crosses to* L *and beckons off*)

OFELIA. Oh, I see. You mean it's all rather vague at the moment?

CLEOFE (*dignified*) Vague, *perhaps*—up to a point.

OFELIA. Oh, how *splendid*, how lovely. How *lovely*, how splendid.

ALBERTO (*not quite sure why all this displeases him*) Well, *I* think it's all rather . . . I dunno. It seems to me—well, a bit *silly* for Francesca to be in such a hurry.

(ADELAIDE *enters* L. *She carries a tray with a pot of coffee and a cup and saucer, which she puts on the table*)

FRANCESCA. Of course, it is. I agree with you, Alberto. (*She moves to the table and pours out a cup of coffee for Alberto*)

(ADELAIDE *exits* L)

CLEOFE (*severely*) There is no question of hurry. It's simply that time is not standing still. There is a time for pears, apples, watering cans. But, in the meanwhile, some people are growing up, even if others aren't.

ALBERTO (*crossly*) What on earth have you put in these tarts, Aunt Cleofe? Oh, I mean, they're very nice, but goodness me, they do seem to stick—(*he points to his throat*) just here.

FRANCESCA (*crossing to Alberto with the cup of coffee; solicitously*) I've made you some coffee, Alberto. You know, the way you like it.

(ALBERTO *takes the coffee*)

CLEOFE (*not to be sidetracked*) Francesca has grown up into a splendid young woman.

OFELIA. That new jacket looks very nice on you, Francesca.

FRANCESCA. Oh, thank you. Do *you* like it, Alberto?

ALBERTO (*not very cheerfully*) M'm? Yes, it's all right. I mean, yes, it looks very nice.

FRANCESCA (*with a note of pleading*) Alberto, surely you're not going to stay away from the picnic this afternoon? We've been every year.

OFELIA. I wish we could, my dear. But, alas. We have things to see to. Excuse me, my dears. Don't stay there dawdling, Alberto.

(OFELIA *turns and exits* R)

ALBERTO. I shan't be long, Auntie. (*He drinks his coffee*) It's been jolly nice here, anyway. Ah, the life I've got to face won't be all sugar and spice. Struggles. Hard times. City life. It gets you down. Wears you out; turns you upside down. Cold little lodgings; stale air; restaurant food the whole time. And all the frightful dirt.

Francesca. Alberto, we're going to take the spirit lamp with us. After lunch we could have a little grog, with pineapple.

Alberto. Hot?

Francesca. Of course. It'll be lovely. And the air's so fresh up there, too. It'll do you good. You look rather tired.

Cleofe (*moving to the table; diplomatically*) It could hardly be a better day for it, all things considered.

(*The* Postman *enters up* r *along the road. He is very old*)

Francesca. It'll be your last day with us. Do you remember it up there? The lovely meadows; all those blue flowers? You'll be glad to look back on it later. And we can talk about—all sorts of things.

Postman (*stopping at the gate*) Excuse me.

Cleofe. Come in.

Postman (*coming in the gate and moving to* r *of Alberto; solemnly*) Good morning, each. There's a telegram. It's for you, Mr Alberto. (*He hands a telegram to Alberto*)

Alberto (*with casual grandeur*) Telegrams, you see. They're beginning now. I thought as much. Thank you. Now, I wonder who on earth it can be from. (*He opens the telegram and stares blankly at it*)

(*There is a pause*)

Cleofe. Is it from the bank?

Alberto (*rising; baffled*) No.

Francesca. Good news?

Alberto. It seems to be from somebody called—(*he reads*) "Miani". (*He thinks*) Miani? (*He shrugs*) But *I* don't know anyone called Miani.

Cleofe. Is it a mistake?

Alberto. Well, it's very odd. It says—(*he reads slowly*) "Consalvo coming to see you tomorrow stop." Consalvo? I don't know anyone called Consalvo. And why should he be coming to see me?

Cleofe. Is that all it says?

Alberto. No. It says—(*he reads*) "Don't worry stop be very careful stop shall also be there myself to hack you up. Miani." Who *is* Miani? I don't know who he is. And why—why should he want to "hack me up"?

Postman (*knowledgeably*) No, Mr Alberto. That reads: "Back you up."

Alberto. Oh, I see. Well, that's better. (*Rather worried*) But why do they tell me "don't worry stop be very careful stop ", I wonder? It must be a joke.

Postman (*gloomily*) Let's hope so, Mr Alberto. I've delivered a lot of them things in my time, and they don't always bode good. Good morning, each. (*He moves slowly to the gate and goes through to the road*)

B

ALL (*ad lib.; rather startled*) Good morning.

ALBERTO. "Don't worry stop be very careful stop." But why *should* I worry? (*Worried*) I—I mean, why should I?

CLEOFE. Alberto. This couldn't be another of your celebrated *scrapes*, I suppose?

(*The* POSTMAN *moves along the road to* R)

ALBERTO. No, no, Aunt Cleofe, really it isn't. I simply don't know who Consalvo and Miani are at all.

(*The* POSTMAN *stops, turns and moves to the gate*)

(*Rather indignant*) And I'd really like to know why a—a city man like myself, a business man, has to be exposed to this—this sort of . . . (*He breaks off*)

POSTMAN (*calling over the gate*) Excuse me, Mr Alberto, did I give you two or only one? Telegrams, I mean.

ALBERTO. Only one. This one.

POSTMAN. There should have been two. Where is it? (*He searches in his pockets*) I know I put it somewhere. (*Crossly*) The number of people who keep getting telegrams these days, you wouldn't think. It wasn't like this in the old days. (*He takes a telegram from his pocket*) Ah. I knew I'd got it. There.

ALBERTO (*moving to the gate*) Give it to me. (*He takes the telegram from the Postman, hastily opens it and reads it*)

(*There is a long silence*)

This—this is from Consalvo.

POSTMAN (*to the Ladies*) He says he's coming tomorrow.

ALBERTO. It says—(*he reads*) "Complete explanation required stop facts known stop." Facts known stop—what does that mean? (*He reads*) "Kindly expect me tomorrow stop Guido Consalvo Nicola Benedè." (*He pauses*) Damn it, I can't . . . Guido Consalvo, Nicola . . . I can't even tell you how many there are of them. And why are they coming here? It's—it's outrageous. (*Optimistically*) Oh, it must be a mistake.

CLEOFE (*severely*) Oh, yes, of course; you're not the sort of person who——

ALBERTO (*moving towards Cleofe*) But no, Aunt Cleofe, I swear I . . .

CLEOFE. —goes from one mess smack into another, are you?

ALBERTO (*reading*) "Facts known stop."

CLEOFE. I expect they are. It's just what might have been expected from the life you've been leading these last few months.

FRANCESCA (*reproachfully*) Aunt!

CLEOFE. Well, well, it's very, very easy to take a wrong turning.

ALBERTO. But, Aunt Cleofe, I swear to you there's *been* no wrong turning. I don't know what "facts known" means. I'm quite innocent. (*With a change of tone*) I think it must be some madman.

CLEOFE (*shaking her head; gravely*) Alberto, my dear boy, we know you.

ALBERTO. "Kindly expect me tomorrow", it says, "stop." Tomorrow? (*He laughs slightly, suddenly relieved*) Well, the poor things. They want me to expect them tomorrow. The poor old things. Tomorrow, I shan't be here to expect anyone. I shall be far away: a mere drop in the great ocean of the metropolis. Poor Consalvo—it's a pity. It's sad to think of him coming all the way here for nothing, whoever he is. (*Confidently*) And time will spread its kindly mantle of forgetfulness over the whole thing. I—I suppose.

POSTMAN (*coming through the gate; genuinely distressed*) Mr Alberto, I'm very, very sorry—(*he closes the gate*) but our office shuts at seven in the evening.

ALBERTO (*cheerfully*) Does it? I'm very glad to hear it.

POSTMAN (*approaching Alberto; apologetically*) What I mean is the telegrams that come after seven we don't get them till the day after. That's to say, the following morning, I mean.

ALBERTO (*loftily*) And what's all that to do with me?

POSTMAN. Well, that's why your telegrams, instead of you getting them last night . . .

ALBERTO (*backing from the Postman in the direction of Cleofe; anxiously*) Last night?

POSTMAN. You've had 'em today; that's to say . . .

ALBERTO (*staring before him*) The following morning.

POSTMAN. Yes, Mr Alberto. It says tomorrow—and it *was* tomorrow, yesterday. But today it's today.

ALBERTO (*at last understanding*) I see. Damn! (*He pauses, looks at the telegrams, then looks instinctively at the high road. To Cleofe*) Did—did you follow that?

(*The* POSTMAN *moves to the gate and goes into the road*)

CLEOFE. Throughout.

ALBERTO (*apprehensively*) It means—Consalvo may be here— any moment. I . . . (*He pauses. Clutching at a hope*) Oh, I'm sure it's just a joke.

(*The* POSTMAN *closes the gate.*
    The COMMERCIAL TRAVELLER *enters on the road from* R *and moves to the gate. He is well-dressed and brisk*)

TRAVELLER (*in a business-like voice*) Good morning. Have I the honour of addressing Mr Alberto Moesse?

ALBERTO. No.

CLEOFE. Yes.

ALBERTO. Yes, I mean. I—I'm Moesse.

POSTMAN (*funereally*) Good morning, each.

(*The* POSTMAN *exits along the road to* R)

TRAVELLER (*advancing briskly through the gate to* R *of Alberto*) Good morning. I was given your address by the District Councillor, a most obliging gentleman.

ALBERTO. What—what is it you want?

TRAVELLER. It is not the first time that the District Councillor has given me his confidence. (*Brightly*) Mr Moesse. May I draw your attention to this? (*He draws a small box from his trouser pocket, with a sudden gesture*)

(ALBERTO *looks terrified and the* LADIES *are startled*)

ALBERTO. Are you Consalvo?

TRAVELLER (*surprised*) No, sir.

ALBERTO. Are you Miani?

TRAVELLER (*disconcerted*) I'm Pakke.

ALBERTO. Pakke? What do you want me for?

TRAVELLER (*nervously displaying the box*) I—I'm travelling in fountain pens, sir. I . . .

ALBERTO (*furiously*) Get out. How dare you! Leave me alone. Get out of here and go back where you came from.

TRAVELLER (*rapidly withdrawing through the gate*) I'm going, sir. I'm so sorry. I'm going.

(*The* TRAVELLER *exits hurriedly along the road to* R)

ALBERTO. How can people have the impertinence to come marching into people's gardens like that, when . . . (*He breaks off*)

(NOEMI *enters by the high road from* R. *She is aged twenty-five and is an elegant young lady wearing travelling clothes*)

(*He stares at Noemi. Troubled*) Oh. Oh, dear.

NOEMI (*moving to the gate*) Good morning, Alberto.

ALBERTO (*greatly baffled*) G-good morning. Hello, Noemi.

NOEMI. Am I in time? I raced here. (*She comes through the gate to* R *of Alberto*) What—whatever's the matter?

(CLEOFE *and* FRANCESCA *watch in some perplexity*)

ALBERTO. I—I'm just surprised, that's all.

NOEMI. Surprised? Didn't you get my telegram?

ALBERTO. No. Yes. I've had two. But—not one from you—I don't think. Here they are. (*He produces the telegrams*)

NOEMI. Let me see. (*She scans the telegrams*) You are a great silly, Alberto. They've written "Miani". It's Noemi. Surely you might have guessed that at least.

ALBERTO. Yes, yes, yes. I—I did almost guess. But I was hoping . . .

NOEMI. Is Consalvo here yet?

ALBERTO (*in anguished tones*) But-but who *is* Consalvo?

NOEMI. You really are an idiot, Alberto. Look, I must talk to

you. (*She glances momentarily at Cleofe and Francesca*) Will you excuse
us for a moment, please?

Cleofe (*frigidly*) With pleasure. (*She crosses to Francesca*)

(Francesca *sits on the bench*)

Noemi (*energetically drawing Alberto up* l) Come over here for a
moment, Alberto. They've found out all about what . . . (*She
whispers rapidly and intently*)

(*Nothing at first is heard of their conversation, then, after a moment
or two, certain rather disturbing remarks are heard, louder than the rest
of their murmured colloquy*)

Cleofe. I said it. I knew it. (*She sits beside Francesca*) I sensed it.

Noemi (*her voice rising slightly*) . . . but I must warn you,
darling, he's absolutely furious. He'll do anything.

Alberto. I refuse to see him. I'm quite innocent. You know
I am . . .

(*They become inaudible again*)

Francesca. Oh, Aunt Cleofe, do you think anything serious
has happened?

Cleofe. What has happened was bound to happen. I sensed it.

Noemi (*louder*) Can't you understand? He's like an absolute
tiger when he's roused. And there'll be that trial as well.

Alberto. *Trial?*

Noemi. Of course there will. The whole thing's a disaster.

Francesca. Oh, why did he ever have to get mixed up with
city people?

Cleofe. I knew it. I sensed it.

Noemi. He'll certainly prosecute. He isn't joking, he means
what he says . . .

Alberto. . . . trying to pretend I'm a criminal now. Is that
what he thinks?

Noemi (*concluding*) He'll be here any minute. There's no time
to lose. Try and think what you're going to say to him. (*She moves
to the gate*) I'll go and watch on the road.

Alberto. Thank you. Yes, do. I . . .

(Noemi *goes out of the gate and watches the road*)

(*He crosses to* c) One moment, Aunt Cleofe, Francesca.

(Cleofe *rises formidably.* Francesca *rises nervously*)

Cleofe. I sensed it. (*She crosses abruptly to the table*)

Alberto. I must just think for a minute. I . . . (*He pauses briefly*)
Look, I *will* come to the picnic with you, Francesca and Aunt
Cleofe. It will do me good. I—the fresh air. I'll be ready in half
a minute, and we can start at once. (*In a pleading whisper*) Francesca, I must get away from these people as soon as possible. I'll

explain later. (*Louder*) We'll take Aunt Ofelia, too. It'll be best. Then we can shut up the house, and everything'll be all right. (*He calls to Noemi*) Excuse me a minute, Noemi, I'm just going indoors for a moment.

NOEMI (*calling*) All right, darling.

(ALBERTO *leaps across the fence and exits* R)

FRANCESCA (*moving* C *and picking up the tarts*) Good morning, Noemi. (*She moves to the table and assembles the things for the picnic*)

NOEMI (*surprised*) Oh! Francesca. It's you. *You're* here.

FRANCESCA (*calmly*) So it seems.

NOEMI. I didn't notice who it was. Well, well, what a strange mix-up. What a small world it is.

FRANCESCA. Aunt, this is Mrs—it *is* Mrs—isn't it now, Noemi?

NOEMI. It *was*, dear. I'm a widow now. Mrs Noemi Bata.

CLEOFE (*coldly*) How do you do?

FRANCESCA. Noemi was my rival for top place at school.

NOEMI (*laughing*) Oh, yes, we hated each other.

CLEOFE. You'll pardon me if I appear to leave you for a moment, won't you?

(CLEOFE *relieves Francesca of the picnic things and exits* L)

NOEMI. But, you know, you're still very pretty, my dear. Enchanting.

FRANCESCA (*bitter sweet*) Oh, but so are you, Noemi. Even now.

NOEMI (*bitter sweet*) You're still not married?

FRANCESCA. No, dear, not yet.

NOEMI. A nice young man, your next door neighbour.

FRANCESCA (*politely*) I suppose he is, yes. I've never noticed. (*With an evident hint of sarcasm*) I suppose you must have met him at the seaside somewhere? On the beach?

NOEMI. Yes, dear. (*With gentle spitefulness*) Darling, you know, you really ought to put your hair up. You'd look much better. Not quite so—well, not quite so countrified, you know.

FRANCESCA. Thank you, I'll think about it.

(*The sound of a motor-horn is heard off* R. *An ancient motor-car enters on the road from* R. *It is driven by the* DOCTOR, *who is aged thirty. He is archly ceremonious in manner and determined at all costs to be gallant and playful.* NOEMI *gets out of the way. The motor-car need not be visible; if it is not seen, a few obvious deletions are necessary in the following speeches*)

DOCTOR (*speaking from the car*) Here we are. Here we are. Here we *are*. (*He gets out of the car and comes into the garden*) Good morning, good morning, fair ladies. I would be very sorry to be late for such an occasion. But, here I am. The mountains await us.

FRANCESCA. We are ready, Doctor.

DOCTOR (*gallantly*) Ah, more radiant than ever today, Miss Francesca. A veritable springtime floweret.

ALBERTO (*off; calling*) We're coming at once, Doctor. Keep the engine running.

NOEMI. Are you going on an outing, Francesca?

FRANCESCA (*coldly*) Yes, a picnic.

NOEMI. Oh, how sweet.

FRANCESCA. I'm so sorry I can't ask you to come with us. But, of course, we've made all the arrangements now—the food, and so on.

NOEMI. Oh, of course, my dear. (*She retires as before to keep watch on the road*)

(CLEOFE *and* ADELAIDE *enter* L. *They carry packages and a picnic basket*)

CLEOFE. Come on. Are we all ready? Bring those things to the motor, Adelaide. Good morning, Doctor. (*She crosses to the gate and moves to the car*)

(ADELAIDE *follows Cleofe and puts the basket and packages into the car*)

DOCTOR (*moving to the car*) Good morning, dear lady.

CLEOFE. Hurry up, Francesca. Shall I sit next to you, Doctor?

DOCTOR (*helping Cleofe into the car*) Mount, dear lady. The barometer points to dry. A light clouding over to the south-west, but inconsiderable in amount. I trust that my raincoat will prove quite superfluous. And, likewise, my little black bag, the doctor's friend.

CLEOFE. What on earth have you brought your little black bag for?

DOCTOR. Prudence is never a vice, dear lady. You might fall into some deep ravine.

CLEOFE. No, I shan't.

DOCTOR. And are you not bringing an umbrella? (*Musically*) One never can tell in the mountains—forewarned is forearmed. (*Coyly*) Have you never heard that before?

CLEOFE. Often.

(OFELIA *enters hurriedly on the road from* R. *She carries some binoculars*)

OFELIA (*not very well pleased*) Oh, dear, oh, dear, what a dreadful muddle and confusion. First Alberto says one thing, then he says another. (*She climbs into the car*)

(*The* DOCTOR *gets into the car*)

FRANCESCA (*calling*) Alberto!

ALBERTO (*off; calling*) Coming!

OFELIA (*in a loud singing call*) Alberto! Albertino! Close the door of the drawing-room!

ALBERTO (*off; calling*) I'm closing it!

(FRANCESCA *crosses anxiously to the fence and waits for Alberto.* NOEMI, *in a state of alarm, suddenly runs in from the road to Francesca*)

NOEMI (*in a whisper*) My God, here he is. Coming down the road.

FRANCESCA. Who?

NOEMI. Consalvo. I don't want him to find me here. Is there another way out?

FRANCESCA. No. But you can go and hide in that place over there. (*She indicates the little low door of the hen-house down* L)

NOEMI. Thank you. He's terrible when he's angry.

FRANCESCA (*pushing Noemi towards the little door*) Quick. Go in there.

NOEMI (*protesting*) But it's a hen-house!

FRANCESCA. Yes, dear. Go on. Good luck.

(FRANCESCA *pushes* NOEMI *into the hen-house, locks the door, gives a sigh of relief and moves* C.

CONSALVO *enters on the road from* R. *He is aged thirty-five and is large, dark and threatening. He comes determinedly in through the gate.*

ALBERTO, *simultaneously, enters precipitately* R *and leaps over the fence on his way to the car. He,* CONSALVO *and* FRANCESCA *suddenly find themselves all face to face. They stop*)

CONSALVO. Does Mr Alberto Moesse live here?

ALBERTO (*rather frightened*) I—don't . . . (*To Francesca*) D-does he live here?

FRANCESCA (*calmly*) Yes, sir, he does live here.

CONSALVO (*savagely*) I've got to speak to him. It's very urgent. I've been travelling ever since yesterday evening. Where is he?

FRANCESCA (*with winning charm*) Are you Mr Consalvo?

CONSALVO. Yes.

FRANCESCA. I think you sent a telegram?

CONSALVO. Yes.

FRANCESCA. Announcing that you were coming?

CONSALVO. Yes.

FRANCESCA (*angelically*) Then Mr Moesse must be at the station waiting for you.

CONSALVO. At the station?

FRANCESCA. Yes, surely.

CONSALVO. But he doesn't know me.

FRANCESCA. No, but he knows everyone else, and so he'd be bound to pick you out. You will be the only one he doesn't know, you see. This is a very small place, sir.

CONSALVO. Where is this station?

FRANCESCA. Take the main road, then to the right, then to the right again, and then ask. It's only about four miles.

ALBERTO (*helpfully*) Less. About three and three-quarters,

Francesca (*moving towards the car; sweetly*) We must be going. Good morning, sir. (*To Alberto. Hostilely*) Come on, you.

Alberto (*to Consalvo, as he cheerfully moves towards the gate and the car*) Good morning, sir.

(Francesca *gets into the car*)

Good morning. (*He gets into the car*)

(*The car, with festive blowing of the horn, exits* l. Consalvo *is about to go on his way, when his attention is drawn to a series of loud knocks from the inside of the hen-house*)

Noemi (*calling*) Let me out. Please, someone. Come and let me out.

(Adelaide *stands in the road, waving to the retreating car.* Consalvo *crosses to the hen-house and throws the door open.*

Noemi *emerges angrily from the hen-house, pulling cobwebs from her dress*)

Consalvo (*stupefied*) Noemi! What on earth were you doing in there?

Noemi (*crossing to* c; *angrily*) Never you mind. Where's that maid?

Adelaide (*coming into the garden; dully*) Yes, ma'am?

Noemi. Where have they gone?

Adelaide (*solemnly*) They've gone to the Madonna of the Mountain, ma'am.

Noemi (*angrily*) Have they, indeed! Then *I'm* going to the Madonna of the Mountain, too!

(Noemi *rushes out of the gate and exits after the car, along the road to* l. Consalvo *stands a moment, dazed, then quickly pulls himself together*)

Consalvo (*shouting*) Are you? Then, by God, *I'm* going to the Madonna of the Mountain as well!

Consalvo *rushes to the gate and exits along the road to* l *as—*

the Curtain *falls*

ACT II

Scene—*An Alpine spot not far from the Madonna of the Mountain. A little over an hour later.*

Down R *there are the ruins of an abandoned hut, an Alpine refuge. Up* LC *is suggested a cliff that drops almost straight down. A little path leads off up* L. *All entrances and exits in this Act are made by this path. There is a mound up* RC *and bushes* R *and* L. *At the back, over the cliff edge, is a wide expanse of sky. A spring of water is presumed to be off up* R.

(See the Ground Plan at the end of the Play)

When the CURTAIN *rises, the stage is empty. The barking of dogs is heard off* L. *After a few moments,* FRANCESCA *and the* DOCTOR *burst on to the scene by the path up* L, *carrying baskets, bags, etc.*

FRANCESCA (*moving up* C) Here we are then, Doctor: here at last. (*She turns, looks off* L *and calls, evidently to others of the party*) Oohoo! Oohoo!

DOCTOR (*also calling*) Oohoo!

VOICES (*off in the distance; calling*) Oohoo—oohoo!

(ALBERTO *enters up* L. *He is heavily laden and is in a bad temper*)

ALBERTO. Yes: oohoo, oohoo. I've never come up here by a worse path in my life before. (*He crosses below the Doctor to Francesca*)

(FRANCESCA *ostentatiously takes no notice of Alberto*)

I'd like to know why on earth you've made us come here? Why couldn't we have gone with the others? They're already there. Look. (*He turns and points off* L) You can see them. They are at the chapel already. Was the picnic supposed to be at the Madonna of the Mountain, or wasn't it? Why have you brought us here? Bullying everyone as usual.

DOCTOR (*turning to them; gaily*) Oh, come—come—come. Come, come. Come.

FRANCESCA (*to Alberto; sharply*) You could have stayed behind, couldn't you? Why didn't you stay and look after your visitors? (*To the Doctor. With extreme kindness*) Do you like it here, Doctor?

DOCTOR (*enraptured*) Enchanting. Absolutely enchanting. A dream. I think that is the word. (*Gallantly*) And doubly enchanting to come hither under the care of a guide so exceptional—so—youngly exquisite, may I say?

ALBERTO. No.

FRANCESCA. Thank you, Doctor.

ALBERTO (*taking a bag from his shoulders*) I should think Aunt

Cleofe must have stuffed a dozen electric irons in this damned bag. (*He throws the bag down to the ground. There is a muffled smash*)

FRANCESCA. May I ask what you think you're doing? (*She picks up the bag and looks inside*)

ALBERTO (*carelessly*)   Something must have happened to something.

FRANCESCA. The rum has gone all over the cold omelette. Oh, how awful! (*She throws the bag down, so that it drops on Alberto's foot*)

ALBERTO (*jumping*)   Well, don't dump the bag down on my foot! You seem to be in a very pleasant mood today, I must say.

FRANCESCA (*pointing off* R)   Doctor, have you seen the spring?

DOCTOR (*crossing* R *and looking off*)   Yes. Charming, quite charming. Such lovely green grass; such velvety moss.

FRANCESCA (*pointing along the back of the stage*)   And the ravine?

ALBERTO. Ravine, my foot! Why, if I went and stood up in it my head would poke over the top.

(FRANCESCA *ostentatiously talks only to the Doctor. She points off* L, *to where the rest of the party has gone*)

FRANCESCA. I think this is far nicer than the other place, don't you, Doctor? You get a much finer view from here.

DOCTOR. Beautiful, beautiful! Picturesque. Yes. (*He points off* R) And what is *that*?

ALBERTO (*crossly*)   That, Doctor, is a mountain. What do you think it is? It's a mountain. (*He moves down* LC, *sits on the ground and unpacks the picnic basket*)

DOCTOR. What a sweeping immensity! So elevating to the thoughts. And the air so healthy, so balsamic. (*Explanatorily*) Owing to the presence of resin.

ALBERTO. In any case, I found this place before anyone else did: years ago, I was thirteen, or fourteen, at the most. (*He spreads out the picnic rug*)

FRANCESCA (*moving to Alberto and assisting him with the rug; coldly*)   You're wrong, Alberto dear. It was I who discovered it first.

ALBERTO. What? Nonsense! Who explored the palace first, me or you?

DOCTOR (*moving up* R)   The palace?

FRANCESCA (*pointing to the ruined hut*)   We call that the mountain king's palace.

DOCTOR. Ah, yes, of course. I understand. The dear games of childhood. How sweet it is to recall them, is it not? And who was the *king* of the castle? (*He moves to the hut*)

FRANCESCA. I was.

ALBERTO. No, you weren't. *I* was.

FRANCESCA. I'm sorry to contradict you, Alberto. *I* was.

ALBERTO. I'd like to know how a woman could be king of the castle. I merely ask.

Francesca. Well, I was: that's all.

Doctor. Perhaps you were *both* king of the castle?

Alberto (*indignantly*) No. *I* was. Whenever we came up to picnic at the Madonna, Francesca and I always brought our basket up here. I was king of the castle. You might just cast your mind back and recall whether or not you were my favourite slave? Were you, or weren't you?

Francesca (*aloofly*) Just as you wish. (*She picks up a glass*) I should hate to upset you.

(Francesca *crosses and exits up* R *to fill the glass with water from the spring*)

Doctor (*examining the hut; funereally*) I suppose this thing isn't dangerous? It seems firm enough. But those cracks provoke a little misgiving, rather.

(Francesca *enters* R *with the glass filled with water*)

Francesca (*moving to the Doctor*) Do taste the water, Doctor. (*She hands the glass to him*)

Doctor. Thank you. (*He sips the water and splutters*) Pooofff!

Alberto. Nice taste, Doctor? Like bad eggs rather, isn't it?

Doctor (*severely*) On the contrary, it's very good for the system. (*He sips gingerly*) Sulphur. (*He sips*) Iron. (*He sips*) And slight traces of arsenic. (*He returns the glass to Francesca*) Very life-enhancing. Ah, what a pity-pity-pity we have no initiative in this country. If only this were America!

Francesca. Don't you think this would be a wonderful place for us to eat?

Doctor. Are we going to eat *here*?

Francesca. Yes. There's no-one to bother us here.

Doctor. I—think it is a little bit cut off, isn't it? Isolated rather? And even a wee bit damp, I fear me.

Francesca (*crossing, kneeling and helping Alberto*) Oh. Doctor, don't tell me you're afraid of the damp.

Doctor. Oh, no, no, I never said that, I never said I was. No, no. (*He points off* L) It's only that over there with the others, it's under cover. Sheltered, as it were. I observe a few little clouds gathering, a few little clouds in the sky. I would not like us to be the victims of one of the frequent mountain deluges.

Alberto (*mischievously*) Doctor, I suppose you wouldn't like to call a deluge down upon us, by your magic arts?

Doctor (*offended*) I am not aware that I command such arts, my friend.

Francesca (*hastily*) Good, then that's settled. We'll eat here. (*She sits above the rug*)

(*The* Doctor *crosses and sits* R *of the rug.* Alberto *sits* L *of the rug*)

(*Casually*) And now someone will have to take the others their part of the cold omelette.

ALBERTO (*suspiciously*) What was that?

FRANCESCA. Their part of it. The whole of the cold omelette is here in the bag. You wouldn't like them all to die of hunger over there, would you? Without any cold omelette?

ALBERTO (*resolutely*) So, that's it. No, I won't. No, no, *no*. I'm not moving from here. Don't think it. One, I'm tired; two, it's too far; three, I don't want a piece taken out of my leg by one of those dogs; four, I'm not moving; five, I . . .

FRANCESCA (*icily*) No one ever expected so unselfish and kindly an action from *you*, Alberto. Why should they? I'm so sorry, Doctor, I'm sure *you* won't mind.

DOCTOR (*sadly*) I—I have to go all the way up there? To take the cold omelette?

FRANCESCA. I'm so sorry. It isn't very far. (*She hands a package to the Doctor*)

DOCTOR (*stoically*) I am ready. (*He rises*) It is a pleasure for me to execute your commands. *I fly!* (*He moves towards the path* L, *then stops and turns*) Oh. Look. Look. Have you noticed?

ALBERTO. What?

DOCTOR. The wind has changed. It has veered round, right round. Dear me. We can no longer exclude the possibility of a storm, I fear. No matter. I fly. I—I suppose those dogs are quite safe?

ALBERTO. Just look them straight in the eye.

(*The* DOCTOR, *with a cold glance at Alberto, exits* L. *There is a renewed barking of dogs as he goes. Cow-bells are also heard*)

DOCTOR (*off; with nervous playfulness*) Down, down, there. Good dog, good doggy-woggy. (*His voice dies away*)

FRANCESCA (*calling*) Thank you, Doctor.

ALBERTO. Francesca.

(FRANCESCA *does not reply*)

Francesca, what's the matter with you today?

FRANCESCA (*contemptuously*) Nothing. It's you who seem upset.

ALBERTO. Can't you understand that that was all nonsense down there? A mistake, that was all. That chap, Guido Consalvo . . . (*He breaks off*) You know, you were quite right to send the silly devil to the station. It was a brainwave. (*He laughs*) When I think of the old boy waiting for me there on the platform, all hot and sticky—and the train going in a few minutes. You know, Francesca, these business men never have a minute to spare. I bet he's got a ticket to America in his pocket for tomorrow. If he doesn't get to the boat in time tomorrow, the ticket will expire. And off he goes, on the ocean wave, forgetting and forgiving. Well, I hope he has a pleasant journey.

FRANCESCA (*bitingly*) And the lady?

ALBERTO. Oh, she'll go with him. You don't want her to settle here for good, do you?

FRANCESCA. Do you know why I helped you? Because I felt sorry for you. You looked so frightened.

ALBERTO. Who? Me? Frightened? I was just holding myself back, that was all. Why, I could have pulverized him there and then—like a fly. I'd just like to meet him again. I'd show him.

FRANCESCA. And I wasn't just sorry, Alberto. I was also pretty disgusted. Do you understand?

ALBERTO. But can't you see that you're wrong about all this? It's all perfectly innocent; it'd win a world championship for innocence. That lady is a widow; one of these extremely correct, irreproachable women. He's her brother, just her brother, that's all. Heaven knows what you've been imagining. There's been a silly little bit of gossip about absolutely nothing, and he's worried about it, that's all. Poor chap. It's all terribly simple and innocent. And tomorrow *he'll* be leaving, and *she'll* be leaving.

FRANCESCA. Are you quite certain of that?

ALBERTO. Did I tell you, or didn't I? They'll be on board ship, and everything will be dead and buried and forgotten? And you turn nasty over a trivial little thing like that. You enjoy ruining my last few hours here; the last moments I shall ever spend here. Ah, there used to be a time when we agreed about everything. You stuck up for me, and I stuck up for you.

FRANCESCA (*mollified*) But, Alberto dear, that was what I was upset about. Surely you realize that? You used to be so frank with me the whole time. You told me everything. Everything. It was always just the two of us against everyone else, whatever happened. Do you really think those two are going away?

ALBERTO (*looking at his watch*) They've already gone, my dear girl.

(*A very distant train whistle is heard off in the valley*)

Did you hear? The train. (*He imitates the train whistle, rises, moves up* C *and looks off as though watching the train in the valley. After a few moments he turns*) And tomorrow I shall be on it, too. (*He imitates the train whistle*) It means good-bye.

FRANCESCA. Alberto.

ALBERTO. Yes?

FRANCESCA. You'll—come back here sometimes?

ALBERTO (*shrugging*) I don't know. Sometimes. Not very often, I'm afraid. (*He sits on the mound up* RC)

(FRANCESCA *rises and takes a step towards Alberto*)

FRANCESCA (*suddenly*) Oooh! (*She clasps her ankle*)

ALBERTO. What have you done?

FRANCESCA. My ankle. Oooh!

ALBERTO. Hurt?

FRANCESCA (*standing on one foot*) Aaah! I can't put my foot down. Oh, Alberto, I think I've sprained it.

ALBERTO (*indifferently*) Yes, it's an easy thing to do, up here.

FRANCESCA (*indignantly*) But, Alberto. Do at least please come and help me.

ALBERTO (*shrugging*) I'm coming, I'm coming. (*He rises and moves to Francesca*) What do you want me to do?

FRANCESCA. You'll have to lift me up.

ALBERTO. Lift you up?

FRANCESCA. Yes. And carry me. I can't put my foot to the ground. You know how it is with a sprain.

ALBERTO. Carry you? Where to?

FRANCESCA (*pointing off* L) Why, up there. To Auntie.

ALBERTO (*calmly*) Oh, no, I shan't. The ground's too uneven. And you're heavier than I am.

FRANCESCA (*indignantly*) You—you refuse? You're going to leave me here?

ALBERTO. Of course, I'm not. I won't leave you. I'll stay with you. You could sit down for a bit, and wait. You'll be quite all right. The doctor will be back any minute. He's a big, hefty chap, and besides, he's used to these things. He's a doctor. He'll carry you. (*He helps Francesca to sit down on the mound*)

FRANCESCA (*after a pause; shuddering*) So you—you'll make the doctor carry me?

ALBERTO. Yes. I was just saying: it's his job. (*He crosses and sits on the ground* L *of the rug*)

FRANCESCA. Ah, yes, it's his job. (*After a pause. Calmly*) Alberto, look. I—I mustn't let the doctor carry me.

ALBERTO. What do you mean—mustn't?

FRANCESCA (*enigmatically*) I mustn't, that's all.

ALBERTO. Why?

FRANCESCA. He would have to put his arms round me.

ALBERTO. Poor him. Well, he's not so ugly as all that.

FRANCESCA. On the contrary, I think he's very handsome.

ALBERTO. Well, there's no need to exaggerate.

FRANCESCA. I think he's a fine figure of a man. (*Modestly*) That's the reason, of course.

ALBERTO. What do you mean—that's the reason?

FRANCESCA. Well, of course. Surely you knew? With things as they are—it really wouldn't be quite nice for him to put his arms around me, just yet.

ALBERTO (*after a silence; rising slowly*) You mean—you and the doctor . . .?

FRANCESCA. I thought you'd probably noticed.

ALBERTO (*crossing to her; surprised and indignant*) You and the doctor—there's a—something—between *you and him*?

FRANCESCA. I don't see what there is to be so surprised about.

ALBERTO (*greatly annoyed*) So that was what your aunt was going on about. (*He sits beside Francesca on the mound*) I see. Since when?

FRANCESCA. Oh, well—it's all rather vague, of course—at the moment. Very little has been actually *said* yet.

ALBERTO. And you really mean to say you—*like* that—that extraordinary *thing?*

FRANCESCA. I certainly don't dislike him. He's—I find him very interesting. I'm not saying he—exactly *thrills* me, of course, but—he's a fine figure of a man. And there's his voice. It's so manly. Aunt Cleofe agrees with me.

ALBERTO (*exploding*) Manly! Manly! The doctor's voice, manly. Why, he talks like this—baa-baa-baa. Like an old sheep— playing a trombone. (*He laughs satirically*) The doctor—handsome. Why, he's like a—I don't know, an old monkey-nut. He's like an old umbrella-stand. He's disgusting. The thrilling doctor! Good heavens! (*He rises contemptuously, moves and stands on the cliff edge up* C)

FRANCESCA (*already sorry*) But I didn't say he thrilled me. You misunderstood me.

ALBERTO (*looking down on her from the cliff*) That was what you said. I've never heard anything like it. It makes me feel quite sick. Here, in my tummy. (*Furiously*) And to think that I've always thought you were a person—above such things. Why, I'm ashamed even to think that you . . . Oh!

FRANCESCA (*in a low voice*) I'm a woman, you know, just like any other woman, Alberto.

ALBERTO. And I'm a fool. Why? Because I liked to think there was at least one girl in the world who was different from all the rest. I see now. I understand. Hence all those little tricks to try and get him up here alone, and send me away.

FRANCESCA (*disheartened*) You know, Alberto, it's just possible you haven't understood *anything at all.*

ALBERTO. I see. I don't understand now, don't I? Very well, I'll go and shout for him. The thrilling doctor. Then he can look after your sprained ankle.

(*The dogs are heard barking off*)

FRANCESCA. No, listen, Alberto.

ALBERTO (*crossing to the path* L) He can carry you up there with his big manly arms around you.

FRANCESCA (*pleading*) No, Alberto, don't. I haven't explained . . .

(ALBERTO *stares off* L)

(*After a pause*) What's the matter?

ALBERTO (*whispering*) Damn it! Damn it! This is persecution. (*He hastily retreats* C) Consalvo is coming up here.

(FRANCESCA, *forgetting her ankle, rises and runs to the path* L *in order to see*)

FRANCESCA (*looking off* L) And Noemi, too. They're together this time. But you said they'd got to catch a boat for America.

ALBERTO. I only meant I was hoping they'd got to. What are we to do? (*Pleading*) Francesca, could you possibly . . .?

FRANCESCA (*maternal and decided*) Yes, Alberto, of course, I could. Leave them to me. I'll look after this.

ALBERTO (*whispering*) Send them away. Send them away.

(FRANCESCA, *limping once more, moves towards Alberto.*
NOEMI *enters hurriedly* L *and rushes past Francesca to* ALBERTO, *who retreats* R. FRANCESCA *stands* C)

NOEMI. Alberto! Consalvo's here: you *must* see him, and . . . (*She breaks off*)

(ALBERTO *rapidly retreats into the hut* R. *He can still be seen by the audience. The barking grows louder.* CONSALVO *is heard protesting off* L)

CONSALVO (*off*) Why can't you keep those dogs off?

VOICE (*off*) They bain't doen nothen. Doan't 'ee go for to tease 'em.

CONSALVO (*off*) Tease them! Good God in Heaven!

(CONSALVO *enters* L, *exhausted and angry. He is looking over his shoulder*)

What sort of person do they think I am? Tease them, indeed! (*He turns and finds himself face to face with Francesca*)

FRANCESCA (*sweetly*) Ah, good afternoon. We meet again.

CONSALVO (*darkly*) Oh. It's you.

FRANCESCA. How are you?

CONSALVO (*breathing heavily*) Dreadful. This heat's absolutely stifling. And the flies won't let me alone. Young lady, it appears it was quite untrue that there was anyone waiting at the station for me.

FRANCESCA (*innocently*) I think you said it was Mr Moesse you were expecting to meet you?

CONSALVO. I don't know who else you thought I was talking about.

FRANCESCA. But I thought you'd let him know you were coming?

CONSALVO (*angrily*) Well, so I had.

FRANCESCA. But where else can he have expected to meet you except at the station? That's what I told you.

CONSALVO. He thought it was safer to run away. Well, he was mistaken, that's all. (*He crosses above Francesca to the mound and sits*)

NOEMI (*moving to Consalvo*) But, Consalvo, do please listen to me. (*She sits beside him*)

CONSALVO. You keep out of this, Noemi. He's run away to the Madonna of the Mountain. That's where he's gone.

NOEMI. But do at least try and keep *calm*. Try and get your breath back.

CONSALVO. I'll get that back after I've caught that man. And I shall catch him. I *intend* to catch him.

FRANCESCA (*moving to the mound; kindly*) Did I hear you say that Mr Moesse had gone to the Madonna of the Mountain?

CONSALVO (*sulkily*) Yes. To the Madonna of the Mountain.

FRANCESCA. And do *you* want to go to the Madonna of the Mountain?

CONSALVO. Yes.

FRANCESCA. Well, that's easy. (*Angelically*) The Madonna of the Mountain is—(*she points upwards and off* L) just up there.

CONSALVO (*rising; horrified*) Up there!

FRANCESCA. Yes, can you see? Just up there, high up, that little white square thing.

CONSALVO (*sadly*) I see it.

FRANCESCA. It's not so very far. Not so far as it looks. The important thing is not to hurry too fast. That's the secret, up in the mountains. (*She sits on the mound*)

CONSALVO. So I've discovered.

NOEMI (*rising*) But, Consalvo, do listen to me . . .

CONSALVO (*moving towards the path* L) Come on, Noemi. I felt a spot of rain.

(CONSALVO *exits* L. *The dogs bark loudly off*)

(*Off*) You silly fool! Why can't you keep the dogs to yourself?

(NOEMI *crosses and exits* L, *leaving her raincoat on the mound*)

VOICE (*off*) I tell 'ee, sir, doan't 'ee go for to tease 'em.

(NOEMI *enters* L, *ignores Francesca, moves to the mound, picks up her raincoat, then moves to the hut*)

NOEMI (*in a low voice*) Alberto. I really can't understand what you're up to, Alberto. I'm not letting you down, I'm helping you all I can. You know I'm for you and against him, but I really can't see why you . . .

(FRANCESCA *rises*)

FRANCESCA (*coming forward; hostile and sarcastic*) What is it you can't see?

(NOEMI *casts a contemptuous glance at Francesca, then addresses Alberto*)

NOEMI. I don't understand, Alberto, why you insist on provoking him like this. It makes him much worse. You know what Consalvo's like. Once he starts he goes on to the end. You know

I'm on your side—but I do think you ought to face up to it and see him; and try and settle things. Especially as I'm here to support you.

FRANCESCA. So that's what you want, is it?

NOEMI. My dear, I really can't see why you have to keep interfering like this.

FRANCESCA. It's you who are interfering with us. We were perfectly happy till you came.

NOEMI. I don't know what business of yours this is.

FRANCESCA. And I don't know who asked you to come here.

ALBERTO (*from the hut; desperately*) Girls, it's coming on to rain.

CONSALVO (*off in the distance; calling*) Noemi!

NOEMI (*calling*) I'm coming! (*To Francesca*) I'm here to stand by Alberto's side, if you want to know.

FRANCESCA. Alberto has no need of anyone like you to stand by his side.

NOEMI. I suppose you think you are enough?

(*It begins to rain. Occasional thunder is heard*)

FRANCESCA. Oh, *I'm* not in the habit of making long journeys in order to protect young men.

NOEMI (*pulling on her raincoat*) And I'm not in the habit of traipsing about over the hills with them and sticking to them like glue.

FRANCESCA. And I don't deceive my relations by sending them on ahead, like some I could mention.

NOEMI. You silly little fool. You empty-headed little idiot. (*With meaning*) I pity *you*, my dear. Just wait till you're told. (*She crosses below Francesca to* L)

ALBERTO ⎫   ⎧(*Desperately*) Girls! You'll get soaked to
          ⎬(*together*)⎨   the skin.
CONSALVO ⎭   ⎩(*Off; calling*) Noemi!

FRANCESCA. Alberto will tell me all about you.

NOEMI (*turning to Francesca; contemptuous, precise and meaningful*) All? Will he? Good. And then perhaps you'll have the sense—to understand *his* position; *my* position; and the position of *both* of us. Good afternoon.

(NOEMI *exits* L. *The thunder dies away and the rain diminishes. The sky is already beginning to lighten. There is a pause.* ALBERTO *emerges timidly from the hut*)

ALBERTO. Francesca.

FRANCESCA (*turning from him*) You fill me with disgust. Go away.

ALBERTO. I only want to explain . . .

FRANCESCA (*fiercely*) Leave me alone. Go away. (*She crosses to the rug, kneels and busies herself with the objects on it, unconcerned*)

ALBERTO. To explain what happened, so that you shan't

think . . . Francesca, it's such a little thing, really it is. You've no idea what a tiny little thing it all is.

FRANCESCA. I wish to hear nothing about it.

ALBERTO (*crossing and standing behind Francesca; becoming more disturbed*) Do you know what it's all been caused by? All this trouble and fuss? People sending telegrams and bothering people like this? It's all been caused by a simple little outing in a rowing-boat; the sea was as smooth as glass. Everyone was rowing on it. In little boats. Is there any reason why I shouldn't have gone out in one like everyone else? That's all it was. A little outing in a rowing-boat. That's all.

FRANCESCA. I've told you I wish to know nothing about it.

ALBERTO. An outing in a rowing-boat. How was I to know that a great typhoon sort of thing was going to blow up before I knew where I was? It was terrible. Winds, waves. Like the end of the world. Like a hurricane. Or a tempest. Why, the boat almost capsized. We might both have been drowned, just like that, swept away. You ought to be glad we escaped. We were like a couple of drowned mice. We might both have caught our deaths, quite easily.

FRANCESCA (*turning slowly and looking at him*) Both of whom?

ALBERTO. Why, I—and that girl, Noemi. (*He kneels to face her*) It wasn't my fault the wind carried us lower down, was it?

FRANCESCA. What do you mean—lower down?

ALBERTO. What do you think I mean? Lower down. Lower down on the beach. A bit of deserted sand; I don't know where it was; it was raining like a tap; thunder and lightning. A flood almost. (*As though he had now told all*) That was all. *That* is my terrible crime.

FRANCESCA. Is that all?

ALBERTO. Of course it's all. I had to pay for the boat as well. (*Angrily*) Did they expect us to stay there on the beach, catching pneumonia? Or waiting to be struck by lightning? Fortunately, there was a large hut. We went inside to shelter.

FRANCESCA. Ah, yes. And then?

ALBERTO. Then nothing. (*He pauses, rises and wanders aimlessly up* c) It was a deposit place for cement and hydraulic lime. That's all. If the people it belonged to hadn't been such fools, nothing would have happened. How could anybody think we'd gone in there to steal cement and hydraulic lime? It's mad. I don't know who it was, but someone heard a noise, and thought there were thieves in the hut.

FRANCESCA (*angrily*) And then?

ALBERTO. Why, they called the police, of course. Can you imagine anything so silly? I can't tell you the stupid things they said, all the lies they made up. Why, we still had them *on*.

FRANCESCA. Had what on?

ALBERTO (*indignantly*) Our bathing-dresses. They said we'd

taken them off to dry ourselves. It just wasn't true. We still had them on. Everything was perfectly in order. How could they expect us to be carrying identity cards and documents in our bathing-dresses? Have you ever heard anything so stupid?

FRANCESCA. Well?

ALBERTO. Nothing. The fool of a policeman telephoned all over the place, and crowds of people came rushing up. Fortunately, we were recognized at once and everything was perfectly all right. (*Virtuously*) Naturally, no one thought *I* was the sort of person that creeps round stealing cement and hydraulic lime.

FRANCESCA (*after a pause; coldly*) What *is* hydraulic lime?

ALBERTO (*impatiently*) I don't know what it is. It's *lime*. Of some sort.

FRANCESCA (*distantly*) Well, you were very lucky.

ALBERTO. Yes, but do you know what happened? The policeman said I'd called him a fool and punched him. Can you imagine me doing such a thing, Francesca?

FRANCESCA. No. What happened then?

ALBERTO (*moving and sitting above the rug; after a pause*) They arrested me.

FRANCESCA. Well?

ALBERTO. They took us away. In our bathing-dresses. When you think about it, well, it would almost . . .

FRANCESCA (*cold and angry*) Make anyone laugh, wouldn't it? Is that what you mean?

ALBERTO (*as though this were unimportant*) They say we shall have to appear in court.

FRANCESCA. In court?

ALBERTO. Oh, it won't be anything important. It shouldn't last more than about three years, they say. Though, of course, there'll be a pile of expenses to pay. No, that's not the trouble.

FRANCESCA. Why, is there something more?

ALBERTO (*as though recounting a complicated but rather amusing and interesting story*) You see, it's Noemi's relations really. They have terribly old-fashioned ideas. They've gone absolutely wild over this. Well, you saw. The extraordinary thing is they're not *her* relations at all, really, they're her husband's relations. She's a widow. He's dead. The whole thing's mad, of course. And these relations . . . Are you listening to me?

FRANCESCA. I'm listening.

ALBERTO. Well, actually, they're also the shareholders in Consalvo's bank. He's a banker, you see. And also he's Noemi's brother. And he's the man who's given me this job in the bank. He's the manager of it.

FRANCESCA (*her head beginning to go round*) The manager!

ALBERTO. Yes, because, you see, Noemi very kindly got her brother to give me this job in his bank. It was she who did that. I was to have started there the day after tomorrow. Or sometime.

But, you see, *now*, Consalvo has gone crazy, too. Because what's happened is that Noemi's late husband's relations—the people I think I told you about, who are so old-fashioned—*they* say that if he doesn't get things cleared up they'll withdraw their capital. Do you follow me? They'll withdraw their capital.

FRANCESCA. Why?

ALBERTO. Because of the newspapers.

FRANCESCA. Newspapers?

ALBERTO. Yes, of course, didn't I tell you? Down there on the beach in the hut some newspapermen came, you see; and so a rumour has got about—a rumour that *they*, the relations of Noemi's late husband, will withdraw their capital; and so the customers of the bank have started to talk and spread rumours, and there's a panic started, and if Consalvo can't get things put straight, they're already saying there'll be a failure.

FRANCESCA. A failure?

ALBERTO. But what on earth should I know about all this? I can't tell you what a mess everything has got into. Noemi is on my side, because she's above all these things, of course; she's a sensible modern woman. Can you imagine what I felt when they took our photograph and published it?

FRANCESCA. A photograph?

ALBERTO. Yes, in the newspapers.

FRANCESCA. In bathing-dresses?

ALBERTO. Yes. But of course, it's all very indistinct in the picture, no-one could possibly tell it was us. If it weren't for . . .

FRANCESCA. Weren't for what?

ALBERTO. Well, how was I to know? I gave them our names and addresses. They printed them, under the photo.

FRANCESCA (*turning away from him*) I think I'm beginning to understand. What happened after that?

ALBERTO. Well, what do you think? Gossip, scandals—cartoons in the papers—and a comic song. They're singing it in one of the revues. (*With sudden anger*) Well, is it fair, do you think? Is it right that Consalvo should chase after me like this and cause all this trouble? Just for a row in a boat.

(*There is a long silence*)

Francesca.

(*There is another silence.* FRANCESCA *has her back to Alberto*)

Francesca, say it if you think it. Am I . . .? Do *you* think I'm a criminal, too?

FRANCESCA (*turning and bending over the provisions*) No, Alberto, you're exactly what you've always been: ever since you were a little boy. And I have always liked you just as you are. Come and eat.

ALBERTO. Eat? But they'll be coming back.

FRANCESCA. Of course. But let's eat. And while we're eating, we can think what we shall have to do. Because it's quite clear I shall have to help you in this, too, Alberto. It's *I* who'll have to get you out of trouble again.

(ALBERTO *stares at Francesca*)

What's the matter? What are you staring at?

ALBERTO. You, Francesca. How very good you are. Yes, certainly, let's eat—and think. (*He removes his jacket*) Look: we'll put my jacket on the ground, shall we? The grass is wet.

FRANCESCA (*affectionately*) Give it to me. (*She takes the jacket from Alberto*) You don't know how to do anything. (*She spreads the jacket on the ground*) Aren't you cold?

ALBERTO. No, no.

(FRANCESCA *and* ALBERTO *sit side by side on the jacket.* ALBERTO *adapts himself with great readiness to the role of spoilt child.* FRAN- CESCA *picks up the flask of rum and a glass*)

FRANCESCA (*handing him the flask and glass; brusquely*) Drink a drop of this.

ALBERTO (*pouring some rum*) You know, Francesca, there are some things you can't understand. (*He drinks*) You're the serious type. In some things you don't even seem like a girl at all.

FRANCESCA (*with lowered gaze*) Don't you think so?

ALBERTO. No. You might be a boy. Now, that woman Noemi's quite diff——

FRANCESCA (*interrupting affectionately*) Don't tell me anything, Alberto. I already know everything. And we have so little time. Consalvo will be back here any minute. And in that little time we have to think of something that will settle things once and for all. Haven't we?

ALBERTO (*happy that someone is looking after him*) Certainly. Sure.

FRANCESCA (*pointing to the tart; maternally*) More tart?

ALBERTO (*graciously*) Just one slice.

FRANCESCA. No, I'll cut it for you. (*Joking, but agitated also*) Aren't I your slave? Your favourite slave?

ALBERTO (*in difficulties with the tart*) The crust keeps breaking.

FRANCESCA (*cautiously*) Alberto, have you any idea what those people really want of you?

ALBERTO (*with his mouth full*) Me?

FRANCESCA. What Noemi meant, for example, when she said you must make up your mind and face up to it.

ALBERTO. Face up to what Consalvo had to say, she meant.

FRANCESCA. And what is Consalvo after?

ALBERTO. Consalvo? Well, *I* think he's out of his mind.

FRANCESCA. No, perhaps not quite out of it. (*She offers him the flask*) A little more rum? Alberto—I'd do anything in the world to get you out of this mess. Do you realize that? And perhaps there is one way. Even if it meant I had to—*sacrifice* myself—I'd do it willingly. Do you remember once? I even lent you some money—which you never paid me back? I'm—very fond of you, Alberto. More than you think. I know that sometimes I'm rude to you; short with you, perhaps.

ALBERTO (*with his mouth full*) It's character, Francesca. It's all a question of character. You know my Aunt Fausta; she's just the same. She's always been absolutely unbearable ever since I can remember. Character, that's what it is.

FRANCESCA (*distressed; earnestly*) But I'm not like that at all, Alberto. My character—is gentle, and submissive, and affectionate.

ALBERTO. Oh, I know. But every so often—bang! And something awful pops out.

FRANCESCA. Oh, Alberto, you mustn't think that. I can't bear it. I'm a good girl, Alberto. I'm cheerful, I'm very fond of—everyone.

ALBERTO (*conceding the point*) Well, who said you weren't? You *are* a good girl.

FRANCESCA (*embarrassed*) I know I'm not a rich girl. That's true; but even that's a good thing sometimes.

ALBERTO. Oh, yes, quite. It moulds people; shapes them.

FRANCESCA. Of course it does. It's meant I've learnt to do things in the house; I'm very good at some of them. You see this jacket? I made it myself. I can't tell you what a bother it was to get right. But I wouldn't change it for that dress Noemi was wearing. It's come out rather well, don't you think?

ALBERTO (*feeling the jacket*) Yes, it looks very well on you. (*He has marked it with jam*) Damn! Sorry. My fingers were sticky from the tart: I've smudged it. (*He attempts to clean it by rubbing it with his elbow*)

FRANCESCA. It doesn't matter, Alberto, don't bother. You'll only make it worse. I'll wash it off at the spring.

ALBERTO. I trail disaster with me wherever I go.

FRANCESCA. But, Alberto, that's what I like about you. Didn't you know? It's rather as though you'd stayed a boy, and only I had grown up. And you ought to realize that. (*Tremulously*) I've never played with any other boy except you, Alberto. Always with you. With you. (*Her voice is shaking and she does not know how to begin*) How—fresh the air is, isn't it? And how lovely and clear the sky is now.

ALBERTO (*without turning round; lazily*) Yes. Lots of country you can see from here, can't you? What a view.

FRANCESCA. Alberto, listen. There's something I wanted to say to you. I wanted to say . . . Give me the flask, will you? (*She takes the flask, pours some rum into a glass, drinks rather liberally, then laughs*) Ah, that's better. It gives you courage, I always think. Strength. (*Determinedly*) Listen, Alberto, you're really a boy, do you see? You're not a bad boy—but you don't think. You say silly things, you tell little fibs. It's because of that that some people think something may happen to you.

Aʟʙᴇʀᴛᴏ (*rather struck*) What sort of something?

Fʀᴀɴᴄᴇsᴄᴀ. I don't know—accidents, designing people. If there's no-one to look after you, who can tell what troubles and disgraces you may get yourself into? Poor Alberto.

Aʟʙᴇʀᴛᴏ. Damn it, Francesca, what an extraordinary way to talk to anyone.

Fʀᴀɴᴄᴇsᴄᴀ. One can put up with other people being unhappy. It's almost natural. But not you. It's so nice to see you happy. To see you suffer must be—I don't know, heartbreaking.

Aʟʙᴇʀᴛᴏ (*simply*) Oh, naturally.

Fʀᴀɴᴄᴇsᴄᴀ. You see, you're so simple and trusting, Alberto. For example, whenever there's any false money in the village, who is it always palmed off on to? You.

Aʟʙᴇʀᴛᴏ. Oh, but I always manage to pass it on to someone else. I'm very good at it.

Fʀᴀɴᴄᴇsᴄᴀ. There ought to be someone near you—to protect you.

Aʟʙᴇʀᴛᴏ. What do you mean—protect me?

Fʀᴀɴᴄᴇsᴄᴀ. It's just that—you'd be better off if there were. And there's your health, too. You're not at all strong, you know.

Aʟʙᴇʀᴛᴏ. Not strong!

Fʀᴀɴᴄᴇsᴄᴀ. No. Anyone can see you lead quite the wrong sort of life. What you need is someone by you to keep you well, and happy, and clean.

Aʟʙᴇʀᴛᴏ (*much offended*) Oh, so I'm not clean now!

Fʀᴀɴᴄᴇsᴄᴀ. No, please try and understand me, Alberto.

Aʟʙᴇʀᴛᴏ. I'm *terribly* clean!

Fʀᴀɴᴄᴇsᴄᴀ (*rather huskily*) Alberto, why don't you get married? (*She pauses briefly*) After all, there comes a time when—naturally, one has to choose very carefully—among the people who are near to one. I know that there—*is* someone, certainly—who—in whom you could have complete confidence, and who has shown in the past how very reliable she can be—and how fond of you she really is.

Aʟʙᴇʀᴛᴏ (*laboriously hunting for a cigarette*) I—I'm not the boasting sort—but as a matter of fact, I get on pretty well with *most* women.

Fʀᴀɴᴄᴇsᴄᴀ. I think it must be—so beautiful to live with some-one forever. To stay and listen to them the whole time. To watch them eat their dinner and drink their coffee afterwards. And to tell them everything that's happened during the day—such lovely evenings together. One would be—so very *happy*.

Aʟʙᴇʀᴛᴏ (*during an acrobatic experiment in lighting a match*) Oh,

I've thought of that, of course, too. People are bound to get married eventually, it's only natural.

FRANCESCA (*huskily*) Alberto. It's quite obvious what that girl Noemi is after. And Consalvo. "Make up your mind", she said. "Get things straight", etcetera. Don't you see?

ALBERTO (*finally lighting the match*) What? Do you mean . . .?

FRANCESCA. However you look at it, there's only one way of getting things straight, so far as they're concerned.

ALBERTO. Oh, I don't really think so, you know.

FRANCESCA. Oh, yes, my dear.

ALBERTO. No, but think—you may be right about Consalvo; but what about Noemi? Good heavens, she laughs at all that sort of thing. She's sophisticated.

FRANCESCA. How simple you are, Alberto. She's a woman.

ALBERTO. But she's on my side. She's my ally.

FRANCESCA. But do you think she hasn't any secret thoughts of her own about you, deep down? If she hadn't she wouldn't have come rushing up here like this. I may be a country girl, but I have my eyes about me. Listen to me, Alberto. They'll both be back in a few moments. It's quite clear what they're after. If they don't find you here, what will they do? Run after you.

ALBERTO (*cheerfully*) Well, I'll run faster, that's all.

FRANCESCA. No, no, no. That's not the way. (*Embarrassment creeps into her voice*) I'm quite sure that what you ought to do is to wait for them quite quietly here; and tell them—something definite—which will settle things once and for all—both for them and for us. (*She stammers*) Before *they* begin talking about marriage, don't you see, you ought to throw it in their teeth from the start. I am here—if you like I'll do it for you, gladly. You must shut them up at once; make them look silly. Like someone running to catch a train and finding it's already gone. Tell them it's useless to make so much fuss. Because you've already—made up your mind.

(*There is a pause*)

ALBERTO (*rising; thoughtfully*) You know—that *is* an idea.

FRANCESCA (*moved and ashamed*) Oh, Alberto, you must understand me. I'm not very good at explaining.

ALBERTO (*moving up* C *and looking off* L; *absently*) Oh, no, you're very good at it. Very.

FRANCESCA. You can imagine how awkward it is for a young woman—to be the one to speak first—in things like this.

ALBERTO (*who has been following his own train of thought*) Yes, I see it all now. All the little manoeuvres, the little subterfuges . . .

FRANCESCA (*overcome with shame*) Oh, Alberto—no, no, no. Those weren't subterfuges. It's just that—when a woman feels fond of someone—she naturally thinks of marriage. Women think of these things from girlhood onwards—having a home and ba—the cradle. It's what we're made for; and sometimes it may be necessary to make things up, so that the man shall understand. It's a thing we have to be forgiven for. It's because women grow fond, Alberto. They—they fall in love.

(*The sound of a bell and then a distant hymn from the Madonna of the Mountain are heard off*)

(*Deeply moved*) It's the benediction, Alberto. Let's kneel down.

ALBERTO. We shall get our clothes dirty.

FRANCESCA (*kneeling*) It doesn't matter. Come and kneel close to me. The Madonna of the Mountain has granted so many people's prayers.

ALBERTO (*moving to Francesca*) M'm? Oh—all right. (*He kneels beside her*)

(*They remain kneeling until the hymn comes to an end. FRANCESCA makes the sign of the cross*)

FRANCESCA. Amen.

ALBERTO (*absently*) What? Oh, yes. Amen. (*He rises decisively*) Francesca, you were quite right to speak to me like that. You've literally opened my eyes for me.

FRANCESCA (*pale*) Really and truly, Alberto? (*She rises*)

ALBERTO. You've made up my mind for me. It shall be exactly as you say.

FRANCESCA (*almost speechless*) Oh, Alberto . . .

ALBERTO. Yes, you've decided for me. How odd I never thought of it myself. It's the one solution that—solves everything. I shall tell Consalvo the minute he comes back. It's no use beating about the bush, is it?

FRANCESCA (*transfigured*) Oh, Alberto.

ALBERTO. After all, men are made for settling down. Especially when circumstances like this—well, almost—insist on it. You know what I mean.

FRANCESCA. Oh, God, how beautiful everything is. I could almost die of happiness.

ALBERTO. After all, people can't stay in a shell forever, can they? You have to think. Work things out. Think of your position, your whole life, your career.

FRANCESCA. Yes, Alberto.

ALBERTO. Yes. And after all, why should I shut my eyes to the fact that the girl's brother is an important bank manager?

FRANCESCA. Wh—wh—whose brother?

ALBERTO. Why, hers—Noemi's. He'll make a splendid career for me. I'll tell him the minute he comes. I'll say to him: "Dear brother-in-law, spare your breath, I thought of it even before you did; you can order the wedding cake at once." That's what I'll say. And so: honour will be restored. The relations pacified. The dead at peace. Consalvo jubilant. And Noemi—poor girl,

what pathetic little shifts and subterfuges she's had to get up to—
telegrams, clambering all the way up here like this. It really has
got a grip on her, hasn't it? Poor little widow . . .

(FRANCESCA, *hardly knowing what she is doing or saying, moves
with a few uncertain steps up* R, *to hide her face from him*)

Where are you going, Francesca?
FRANCESCA. I—I'm going to—I—I want—to wash my jacket.
ALBERTO. How sensible you are, Francesca. I might never
have thought of it myself. It was very clever of you. It's just like
mathematics, really—the position, the bank, the relations, the
rowing-boat, Consalvo getting so angry—it all fits in, doesn't it,
just like a jig-saw puzzle? I'm not all that enthusiastic about
Noemi, of course, but when all's said and done, she *is* a lady, she
wears awfully nice clothes—and she must be quite well off, too.
Yes, my dear Francesca, we all have to pause and think sometimes; and marriages of convenience—they're called that, you
know—have always been the best. Youth doesn't last for ever.
(*He looks closely at her*) What's the matter? You crying? Because of
the jacket?
FRANCESCA (*trying to restrain her tears*) I was thinking—everything has been so beautiful—I keep thinking of how happy we've
been.

(ALBERTO *moves to Francesca, puts an arm affectionately round her
shoulders and shakes her*)

ALBERTO. You're feeling all right, aren't you? You haven't
had too much of that rum?
FRANCESCA. No, no.

(ALBERTO *leads* FRANCESCA *to the edge of the cliff up* L. *The sun
has begun to set*)

ALBERTO. Look. What a wonderful sky it is, isn't it? You
know, Francesca, life isn't such a bad thing after all. What
colours. (*He calls suddenly*) Noemi-i-i! Noemi-i-i-i! There they are.
Give me that. (*He snatches Francesca's coloured handkerchief from her
shoulders and waves with it. He calls*) Ye-es! We're he-re! Come
ba-ack! (*To Francesca*) I'll speak at once, and get it over. It's much
the best thing. (*He calls*) Come he-re! Yes, they're coming. Good.
Oh, Francesca, we shall have such a lovely house—and who'll
come and see us every now and then? Our dear little Francesca,
Aunt Cleofe the second, eh? (*He calls*) Oohoo! Oohoo! (*To Francesca*) Oh, Francesca, you don't know how fond I am of you, old
boy. We'll invite you to come and stay with us whenever you
like. And to the wedding, of course. Because actually all this is
really due to you, you know. (*He calls*) Oohoo! Oohoo! Oohoo!

(FRANCESCA, *in the extremity of despair, seems undecided whether
to burst into sobs or to throw herself over the cliff. Instead she suddenly*

pushes ALBERTO *over the edge with both her hands. He disappears immediately.* FRANCESCA *is at once filled with wild distress and falls on her knees, bending over the edge)*

FRANCESCA (*in terror*) Oh, my God! (*To herself*) What have I done? I didn't mean to. Oh, God! (*She calls*) Alberto! Alberto! Are you all right? (*To the mountain*) Help! Help! Come quickly. (*She leans over the edge*) Alberto, my own Alberto. Please. Alberto. Please try and climb up. Do try.

ALBERTO (*off; in a distant muffled voice*) I might have been killed.

FRANCESCA (*calling*) Help! Doctor! Help! Yes, come up here! Gently, Alberto: steady. Here! Hold on here. Give me your hand.

(ALBERTO's *head appears over the edge*)

Hold me tightly. Up—up. Oh, Alberto. Oh, my dear. Please. Please speak to me. Answer me.

(FRANCESCA *helps* ALBERTO *over the edge. His face and hands are covered with scratches, his mouth full of dirt*)

ALBERTO (*spluttering*) You are a stupid clumsy girl, Francesca. (*He is clearly unaware that she has actually pushed him over*) You brushed against me. You're always the same. You never notice what you're doing or where you're going. I might have hurt myself.

FRANCESCA (*faintly*) Oh, Alberto, what a terrible thing. Have you broken anything? How do you feel?

ALBERTO. It was full of nettles.

FRANCESCA. Don't talk. Lie down here. Here. Keep still; and quiet.

ALBERTO (*beginning to feel frightened*) M-m-must I lie down?

FRANCESCA. Yes, it'll be safer.

(ALBERTO *lies on the ground at the cliff edge*)

Tell me: can you feel anything?

ALBERTO. No. Nothing. (*He winces*) Ooh!

FRANCESCA. Oh, dear. (*She calls*) Doctor! Help! Quick! Help! Doctor!

ALBERTO. Fran-cesca, don't do that. You frighten me as well.

FRANCESCA. Keep calm. Darling, try—try and move your toes, if you can. Can you?

ALBERTO. Yes—I can.

FRANCESCA. Thank God! It means your dorsal column is intact.

ALBERTO (*terrified*) What? Good heavens! Ooooh!

FRANCESCA (*calling*) Help! Wait: there's the doctor's bag.

(*She runs to the rug, picks up the Doctor's bag and runs back to Alberto with it*) I'll bandage you.

ALBERTO (*nervously*) Bandage *what*?

FRANCESCA. I don't know. Your face. There's blood on it.

ALBERTO. Blood!

FRANCESCA. Keep still.

ALBERTO. Oh, God, what's going to happen to me? What's going to happen to me?

FRANCESCA (*energetically slapping plasters on to his face*) Do you feel better like that? M'm?

ALBERTO (*unable to speak plainly because of a plaster across his mouth*) I—don't know—what will become of me?

(*The* DOCTOR *enters* L)

DOCTOR (*panting*) Calm, calm, calm. Keep quite calm. (*He moves to Alberto*)

FRANCESCA. Oh, Doctor, thank God you've come.

DOCTOR. Keep calm. (*He feels Alberto's pulse*) Courage, Alberto. We're here. Look up. Open the eyes. Look up. Quietly.

(*Night is beginning to fall*)

FRANCESCA. Please, Doctor, do do something.

DOCTOR. Quiet-ly. Don't be afraid, my dear, have no fear. I've seen far worse than this in my time. I've seen men smashed up completely. Like pulp. Some of the cases I've been called into have been all to pieces; literally in pieces. Do you know I once saw a man with only half a . . .

FRANCESCA. Oh, Doctor, no, don't.

DOCTOR. I thought nothing of it. Where's my bag? Can he speak?

FRANCESCA. He could till a few moments ago.

DOCTOR. Well, why can't he now?

ALBERTO (*spluttering*) The p—laster . . .

DOCTOR (*shouting at Alberto*) Alberto! Can you hear me? Eh? Can you speak? What happened? Did you fall? Over the cliff?

(ALBERTO *mumbles*)

He says "yes". Good. Excellent. Excellent. Now: let's see.

(OFELIA *bursts in* L)

OFELIA (*loudly*) Alberto! My Alberto! Oh, the poor lamb! (*She moves behind Alberto and bends over him*) Can you hear me, Alberto? It's me: your Aunt Ofelia. Say you can hear me. (*Much louder*) Tell me you can hear me!

ALBERTO (*lifting up one of the plasters; annoyed*) Of course I can hear you! Don't make all that noise.

DOCTOR. Quiet-ly. Breathe in. Breathe out.

OFELIA. Doctor, Doctor: tell me how he is.

(*The* Doctor *gives a series of professional examination grunts, during which the others listen in religious silence*)

Doctor (*rising; with disgust*) Why, he's as well as I am.

Alberto (*rising; anxiously*) I shan't suffer from delayed cerebral shock, shall I?

Ofelia. Or internal concussion, will he, Doctor? That's worse, far worse.

(Cleofe *enters* l)

Cleofe What a lot of nonsense. I told you there was nothing the matter.

Ofelia (*with enigmatic calm*) Oh, no. Nothing. Nothing. Just a little fall over a cliff.

Cleofe (*approaching and looking over the cliff*) Cliff! It's just a ditchful of nettles.

Ofelia. It was a cliff! Suppose he'd bounced!

Cleofe. Well, he isn't a rubber ball, is he?

Ofelia. We should have a corpse at our feet.

Cleofe. He oughtn't to drink so much rum. (*She moves to the mound*)

Ofelia. There was no question of rum. (*Her voice becomes solemn*) Luckily, I was there. With *these*. Alberto's late uncle's marine binoculars.

(*A silence falls. They all turn to* Francesca, *who stands* l *of the cliff, absent and indifferent, apparently staring into the distance*)

Francesca: perhaps you can tell us how Alberto fell over that cliff?

Francesca (*absently*) I pushed him over.

Alberto. *Eh?*

Ofelia. And why did you push him over?

Francesca (*absently*) I just wanted to push him over, that was all.

Ofelia. Dear Alberto, she wanted to kill you. I saw it all. With my own eyes. (*She indicates the binoculars*) And these.

Alberto. She wanted to . . .?

(Noemi *enters suddenly* l)

Ofelia. She wanted to kill you; yes.

Alberto. But why? Why?

Noemi (*calmly and spitefully*) Why? Why, because she's in love with you, darling. (*She moves to Alberto*) She's wildly, madly in love with you.

Alberto (*flabbergasted*) Eh?

Noemi. She loves you. Hopelessly, of course. She loves you—and we all know what she is—a little girl from the country whom no-one pays any attention to, and who doesn't know how to dress, and hasn't a penny in her pocket . . .

CLEOFE (*indignantly*) She has an insurance policy which matures the minute she's sixty-five.

NOEMI. A little snake in the grass—and *very* hypocritical, and *very* calculating, and very, *very* jealous . . .

(ALBERTO, *suddenly wild with anger, tears off his last bandages*)

ALBERTO. If you dare say another word against that girl, I'll slap your face.

(CONSALVO *enters* L)

If you want to know . . .

CONSALVO (*extending a finger towards Alberto*) If *you* want to know, sir, people can't go on trying to take in other people forever. (*Solemnly*) Are you, or are you not, Mr Alberto Moesse?

(FRANCESCA, *at this point, is near the path* L, *masked by Consalvo*)

ALBERTO (*beside himself with rage*) Yes, sir. I am!

(FRANCESCA, *in the dusk, exits quietly and unobtrusively* L)

I am, and I warn you, for your own sake, to get from under my feet! Get out of my way. (*He pushes Consalvo aside*) Francesca. (*He looks around. Surprised*) Francesca, where are you? Francesca!

(*But Francesca has disappeared*)

DOCTOR
CLEOFE }(*together; ad lib.*){ Francesca! Where has she gone? Francesca. Francesca, where are
OFELIA you? Etc.

DOCTOR (*politely*) I have the most melancholy forebodings, you know.

(CLEOFE, OFELIA *and the* DOCTOR *scatter and look for Francesca*)

CLEOFE
DOCTOR }(*together; ad lib.*){ Look for her. Call her! Francesca! Francesca! Oh, my God, how
OFELIA dark it's getting. Francesca! Etc.

ALBERTO (*to Noemi and Consalvo; with tears in his voice*) If anything happens to that girl, I'll kill you!

(NOEMI *and* CONSALVO *stare in rigid amazement*)

I'll kill you both! (*He calls*) Francesca!

(ALBERTO *exits* L)

(*Off; calling*) Where are you? Answer me. Francescaaaaaa . . .

The stage is almost completely dark. ALBERTO's *voice dies away in the distance as—*

the CURTAIN *falls*

ACT III

SCENE—*A room in the house of a local peasant. A few hours later.*

It is a small, sparsely furnished room. R of the back wall is a door leading to a cow-shed. There is a lunette, or grille, over the door, through which it is possible to look into the room. Back L there is a large open fireplace with a glowing fire. In front of the fire there is a small low clothes-horse on which Francesca's jacket is inconspicuously hung to dry. A rustic settle with sides stands R of the fireplace. A large broom leans against the back of the settle. Below and L of the fireplace is a Windsor chair. The curtained window is L. Below the window is a doorway, without a door, leading to a porch and the outer door off L. A door down R gives access to the kitchen. A primitive dresser stands against the wall R. There is a kitchen table RC with chairs above and R of it. At night the room is lit by a shaded pendant C with the switch above the door down L.

(See the Ground Plan at the end of the Play)

When the CURTAIN rises, it is night, the window curtains are closed and the room is in darkness except for the glow of the fire. It is raining. A knocking is heard on the outer door off L. There is a pause; then the knocking is repeated.

ALBERTO (*off L; knocking violently and calling*) Hi, there! Is anyone in? Open the door, please, will you?

(The FARMER, a young man, enters R, crosses to L, switches on the light and exits by the porch to open the outer door.

ALBERTO enters down L. The FARMER follows him on. ALBERTO is soaked to the skin. He stands LC. The FARMER laughs without apparent reason)

FARMER (*innocently*) Is it raining, sir?

ALBERTO (*after a withering glance at the Farmer*) Have you seen a girl? Francesca, her name is. A dark girl, rather pretty, in a blue dress and a white jacket. (*He moves to the table and looks around, without, however, noticing the fireplace*)

FARMER (*moving a few paces down LC; thoughtfully*) A—a girl, you said, sir?

ALBERTO (*furiously*) Yes, a girl.

FARMER. Yes, I see, sir. What would she be doing?

ALBERTO. How should *I* know? She's been seen near here.

FARMER. Where was she going, sir?

ALBERTO. If I knew, I wouldn't be here asking you.

FARMER. In a blue dress, did you say, sir?

ALBERTO. And a white jacket.

FARMER. I'll go and ask the wife, sir. (*He crosses to the kitchen door and turns*) Would you be the girl's father, sir?

ALBERTO (*outraged*) Father! I—I'm a friend of hers.

FARMER. Ah, yes, I see, sir. A friend. I'll just ask the wife, sir.

(*The* FARMER *exits to the kitchen.* ALBERTO *looks around and suddenly observes Francesca's jacket. He moves to the fireplace, seizes the jacket, runs to the kitchen door, stops and listens, then goes quickly to the fireplace and replaces the jacket.*

The FARMER *re-enters* R. ALBERTO *assumes a nonchalant air*)

No, sir. She hasn't. My wife says she hasn't seen any girl around this way, Sir. (*He moves to* R *of the table*)

ALBERTO (*who has expected this*) Well, well, never mind. I didn't really expect she would have. (*He looks around*) And how has the hay done this year?

FARMER (*looking distrustfully at Alberto*) Well—it might be worse, sir. It doesn't do to complain. My wife wondered if you'd looked over the Lame Goat, sir? That cliff just the other side of the road. There's a sheer drop there, forty feet or more. You never know what's going to happen there, when the weather's like this. The path's very slippery, you see. Poor girl. Let's hope—well . . .

ALBERTO. Let's hope, yes. (*Anxious to linger he points towards the door of the cow-shed*) And the cows this year, the milk, and so on, how's all that done?

FARMER. Well—it might be worse, sir; it—it . . .

ALBERTO (*moving above the table; cheerfully*) Doesn't do to complain, does it?

(*The sound of a motor horn is heard off* L, *followed by violent knocking at the outer door*)

CONSALVO (*off* L; *calling*) Open the door, please. Do you mind opening the door?

ALBERTO (*pointing to the kitchen door*) Could I slip out that way?

FARMER. Well, that just leads into the back-yard, sir . . .

ALBERTO. Good. Thank you: good evening. (*He moves towards the kitchen door*)

FARMER. 'Evening, sir.

(*The* FARMER *crosses and exits by the porch*)

(*Off*) Who is it?

CONSALVO (*off*) Friends, my good man, friends.

(ALBERTO, *instead of going out of the kitchen door, turns and tiptoes to the door of the cow-shed. He opens it and slips inside. Eventually, his curiosity compels him to clamber up to the barred lunette above, where his face becomes visible from time to time.*

CONSALVO *enters* L. *The* FARMER *follows him on*)

FARMER (*crossing to* C) Come in, sir, come in. What dreadful weather.

CONSALVO (*in the doorway* L; *peremptorily*) Look, my good man, have you seen a girl anywhere round here? A rather tall, good-looking girl, in a white jacket and a blue dress?

FARMER. A girl?

CONSALVO. Yes, yes, a girl. A girl.

FARMER (*laughing for no apparent reason*) A blue dress?

CONSALVO (*moving to the settle; irritated*) Yes, blue, blue. That was what I said. Blue. Francesca, her name was.

FARMER. Oh: let's hope it still is, sir. I'll go and ask the wife. (*He moves to the kitchen door, opens it and calls*) Seen a girl, Mrs? (*He pauses*) No? No. (*He turns to Consalvo*) No, sir, she says she hadn't seen any girl like the one you say, sir. (*He closes the door*)

(NOEMI *enters* L)

CONSALVO (*threateningly*) Young man, that girl was seen coming in here.

FARMER (*plaintively*) In here, sir? Why, sir, how can you think —why, sir, may I lose my sight-and-speech if ever I . . .

NOEMI (*moving a few paces towards Consalvo*) Well, before that happens, would you be so good as to tell the young lady that her friend Noemi Bata is here, and it's extremely important that I should speak to her; that is—(*loudly*) unless the young lady has some reason for being ashamed, and feels she ought to hide.

(FRANCESCA, *who has evidently been hiding behind the kitchen door, enters* R, *prepared for battle*)

FRANCESCA (*crossing to* L *of the table*) And why should I be ashamed, or try to hide, may I ask?

(*The* FARMER *withdraws and exits strategically to the kitchen*)

CONSALVO (*aggressively*) What else are we to expect from behaviour like this, young lady? (*He moves above the table. With intense fury*) Young lady: I'd like you to know that I'm a man with a great deal of very important business on my hands; my time is precious. At this moment I ought to be hundreds of miles away from here, sitting at a desk with five telephones on it, and a crowd of extremely important and very touchy business gentlemen waiting to see me. Do you know why I'm here, instead, soaking wet, worn out, and nothing to eat since first thing this morning? (*He breaks off and begins afresh*) Listen: you've read or heard about the famous little mouse, haven't you? The dear little, sweet little, classic little mouse; who gets stuck in the wires at the power-station and puts a whole city out of action? Paralyses trains and factories and central heating and bells and trams all over the whole capital. Well, that's what your friend has done for me. (*He gets steadily angrier*) One day *he* comes on the scene: and the staggering capacity he's shown for bringing calamity on everyone from every single thing he does, has something quite fantastic about it. He's run amok over everything, everything we had in the world; like a bull, let loose in a china-shop.

FRANCESCA. A bull, or a mouse, sir?

CONSALVO. The name of the animal is of no moment. My sister and I, in the vortex of disaster that young man has thrown us into, my poor sister and I decided to choose the lesser of two evils in the hope of straightening things out . . .

NOEMI. Consalvo . . .

CONSALVO. This is no time for delicacy, my dear. My sister might have agreed to sacrifice herself, if it were not for what has happened today: your thoughtless and highly significant gesture —ah, um, *action*, committed against the person of Mr Moesse, made it clear that a situation existed of which we were unaware —a delicate situation, compelling us to conclude that you yourself entertain a certain interest—that is to say, ah, certain feelings for the—the individual aforesaid.

FRANCESCA (*calmly*) The interest I entertain for the person you—refer to is one of the most complete indifference.

CONSALVO (*after a pause*) You speak very definitely on that point. Is that the truth?

FRANCESCA. Of course.

CONSALVO. Ah. I see. (*Gravely*) In that case perhaps I can see about drying my feet. (*He retires to the fireplace, sits on the settle and dries his feet*)

FRANCESCA. You can keep him, Noemi. He is all yours. (*She moves and sits R of the table*)

NOEMI (*crossing to L of the table; innocently*) What on earth are you talking about? (*She puts her handbag on the table, removes her mackintosh and scarf and puts them over the arm of the chair above the table*) Really! Do you think he's—amusing? The right sort, would you say?

FRANCESCA (*spitefully*) My dear, it depends entirely on what you think you can get used to.

NOEMI (*looking idly in her handbag for her mirror; agreeing*) Oh, yes, of course. No-one's going to pretend he's very striking in any way.

FRANCESCA. Good heavens, no. Poor boy, he's terribly country-bred, to put it mildly. He's really only happy when he's gnawing a leg of chicken held in his fingers, or sitting about in his shirt-sleeves.

NOEMI (*inspecting herself in her mirror*) Well, that's not a crime.

FRANCESCA. And physically, of course . . .

NOEMI. Oh, I agree, he isn't much to . . .

FRANCESCA. Not much to write home about, no. And a bit sloppy, of course, most of the time. As for his brain-power . . .

NOEMI. Pretty ordinary that, I'd have said.

FRANCESCA. Almost non-existent. (*In a single breath*) He's suffered from chilblains ever since he was a child; Aunt Ofelia says he snores; Aunt Cleofe calls him a turnip; and he's putting on weight, rather, now—(*after a brief pause*) though, all told, he isn't too bad, I suppose.

NOEMI. All the same, he isn't exactly your ideal, is he?

FRANCESCA. Good heavens, no. God forbid!

(*The cows have begun to sound rather restless*)

NOEMI (*replacing her mirror in her bag*)   Oh, my dear; if you only knew what a weight you'd lifted from my mind.

FRANCESCA (*suspiciously*)   Why?

NOEMI. I was afraid Alberto rather attracted you. I was feeling rather guilty.

FRANCESCA. Guilty? What for?

NOEMI (*closing her handbag with a snap*)   Well, because, you see —I like Alberto very much indeed.

FRANCESCA (*rising; indignantly*)   But you just said you thought he was a terribly commonplace young man.

NOEMI (*triumphantly, and very spitefully*)   But that's just the very reason, my dear. All I meant was—he's a *good* boy; he'll never be one of those big neurotic types; and he'll make a delightful companion. (*As though revealing a secret*) I've lived a little longer than you, Francesca; and I have to confess that I find Alberto enchanting. He's so stupid. And so sly, and even deceitful, at times—and yet, somehow, so sincere, in his own way. I dare say the overbearing, worldly, cynical type of man may seem very attractive to a country girl; but I'm a woman. And in any case there must be a certain amount of honey in Alberto; or there wouldn't be so many flies buzzing round him. His wife will have to be very careful. (*She pauses briefly*) And I—*shall* be careful, my dear. (*She picks up her scarf and mackintosh*)

(*There is a pause*)

FRANCESCA (*backing a few paces; angrily*)   You mean you're going to marry him?

NOEMI. Well, what do you think? I adore him.

FRANCESCA (*very spitefully*)   Well, at your time of life, I suppose it's understandable. When there's no roast beef available, we have to make do with a turnip.

NOEMI (*not pleased*)   Francesca; while we're on the subject: weren't *you* in love with Alberto once upon a time?

FRANCESCA. With Alberto? *Me?*

NOEMI. Yes. Don't you remember the things you used to say about him at school? You said you'd die, without Alberto? M'm? Didn't you?

FRANCESCA. My dear, I was a little girl then. I didn't know him properly in those days.

NOEMI. Do you think you know him properly now? My poor dear Francesca; it's not the same man. The boy who whispers sweet nothing into the ears of schoolgirls isn't the same person as the man who has breathed the fragrance of a full-grown woman, No, you don't know Alberto. He can be jealous; did you know that? He can be a bit of a tyrant, a bully. Because you see, dear: he loves me. That's what it is. He loves me.

FRANCESCA (*who has been much pained by these words*) I don't believe it. It's a pack of lies.

NOEMI. I wouldn't like you to suffer from a broken heart. He loves me.

FRANCESCA. Alberto isn't that sort.

NOEMI. No, I know: you think he's a turnip. A young man can always be a turnip when he wants to. (*She moves towards the settle*)

FRANCESCA (*furiously*) What do you mean?

NOEMI (*turning* C) When a woman means nothing to him. And suffers. It must make him laugh, rather, don't you think?

FRANCESCA. I don't know what you mean.

NOEMI (*depositing her scarf and mackintosh beside Consalvo on the settle*) But it's written all over your face, dear. I can just see the two of you: you, pestering him with little presents and cakes and woollies: and Alberto as cold as an icicle. You shouldn't have been so pressing, perhaps, dear; you ought to have held off a bit more. (*She moves to the table and picks up her handbag*) Still, what can one do when one's in love? One can suffer horribly, I know. I understand just how you feel. And then, after all that. To see him married to someone else.

(*There is a long pause.* FRANCESCA *stands breathing hard for a moment, uncertain whether to burst into tears or to seize Noemi by the hair. Suddenly it flashes on her that there is another way of discomfiting her adversary, and she becomes calm again*)

FRANCESCA. Well, if you really have seen all that's been going on, I suppose it's useless for me to try and keep my secret any longer.

NOEMI. What do you mean?

(CONSALVO, *perturbed, rises*)

FRANCESCA. Well, just *that*: Alberto did see that I was in love with him.

NOEMI. Well?

(ALBERTO'S *face appears at the grille*)

FRANCESCA. He—took advantage of the fact.

NOEMI. What?

FRANCESCA. He took advantage.

(*There is a pause, followed by an intensified, disturbed mooing from the cow-shed.* ALBERTO'S *face vanishes*)

Consalvo (*moving down* lc; *violently to Noemi*)   I said it. Didn't
I? I said it myself. I said I didn't like the young man. You've
always had a weakness for these Bohemian types, Noemi.

Noemi. And do you really think I'm going to believe a piece of
nonsense like that, Francesca?

Francesca. You don't believe it?

Noemi. Of course I don't. I'm not a fool.

Francesca. You don't believe that Alberto and I . . .?

Noemi. It's a stupid lie.

(Francesca *is determined by now to invent any absurdity in order
to defeat her rival*)

Francesca. Very well, since you insist, I shall have to tell you
everything; though God knows I've never wanted to tell anyone.
These—things—as we all know—often have their Fatal Consequences. So did this. Yes. (*She delicately indicates the length of a
rather well-grown baby*)

Consalvo (*moving to the fireplace; pushing his hands through his
hair*) My God!

(*There are renewed bellowings from the cows*)

Francesca. That puts a stop to your little schemes, doesn't it,
Noemi?

Noemi. It's a silly, outrageous, childish lie. You make me
laugh. You're just making it up to try and make things difficult
between me and Alberto.

Francesca. I am a victim, and I have my rights.

Noemi. It's not true, it's not true!

Francesca. We shall see.

Noemi. We'll ask Alberto!

Francesca. Ask him by all means.

(Consalvo *wanders up and down between the fireplace and the
doorway* l, *his hands in his hair*)

Consalvo. My God, what a hell of a mess!

(*The cows bellow still louder.
The* Farmer *enters by the kitchen door*)

Farmer. Please, please, ladies and gentlemen, you're frighten-
ing my poor cows. It'll turn their milk.

(*The* Farmer *exits to the kitchen*)

Noemi (*moving below the table; to Francesca*) You're a little liar.

Francesca (*moving to* r *of Noemi*) He seduced me. He knows
where his duty lies.

Noemi. It's not true. Alberto loves me. Al——

Francesca. Alberto . . .

CONSALVO (*moving to the settle*) Alberto! Alberto! What in God's name ever brought him across my path?

(*The noise has risen to a climax. Suddenly they all turn to the doorway* L.
CLEOFE *enters* L, *shutting a groaning umbrella.*
OFELIA, *who is completely bewildered, follows her on*)

CLEOFE (*with a few paces towards the settle*) May I ask . . . Oh, Francesca, thank goodness you're here. May I ask what that fool of a boy is up to?

OFELIA (*leaning wearily against the door jamb*) Oh, please, *don't* refer to my neph——

CONSALVO (*moving to* R *of Cleofe*) Of whom are you speaking, madam?

CLEOFE. Why, Alberto, of course.

CONSALVO. And why have you come to look for him here?

CLEOFE. Don't be ridiculous! He came in here. He told us to wait for him a moment down at the cross-roads. We've been waiting there half an hour in the pouring rain. (*She moves to the fireplace, beckoning to Ofelia to join her*)

(OFELIA *crosses to the fireplace.* CONSALVO *has understood. His eyes turn to the cow-shed door.* FRANCESCA *backs towards the kitchen door.* NOEMI *backs a few paces down* C. *The cow-shed door is clearly visible. The mooing ceases. There is a tense pause. Suddenly the tiny wail of a new-born calf is heard.* CONSALVO *marches determinedly to the door of the cow-shed and throws it open.* ALBERTO *is still clinging to the bars of the grille. His feet are not touching the ground*)

OFELIA (*faintly*) Alberto.

CONSALVO. Come down, Mr Moesse. And stop molesting those poor unfortunate animals.

ALBERTO (*dropping to the floor; stiffly*) I—I couldn't find my hat. (*He comes a few paces into the room. A certain amount of straw clings to him*)

CONSALVO (*moving close to Alberto; cold and angry*) Never mind about your hat, for the moment; leave it. I wish to speak to you. (*He lowers his voice a little*) Now, sir; what is this extraordinary tale we hear? Is it true that you have misbehaved yourself with this young lady?

(ALBERTO *turns towards Francesca and gives her a look of understanding, then turns to Consalvo*)

ALBERTO (*martyred and stoical*) I cannot deny it, sir.

OFELIA. What nonsense! Alberto *couldn't*!

CONSALVO (*sceptical*) And is it true that there have been—um, ah—Fatal Consequences?

ALBERTO (*even more stoically*) I cannot deny it, sir, I know where my duty lies.

Consalvo (*fiercely*) Then it's quite clear you and your friend must think I look like an imbecile.

Alberto (*lost in thought*) I cannot deny it, sir.

Consalvo. You listen to me. I did first of all think, since you are now an employee of my bank, of sending you to our branch in Madagascar.

Alberto. Madagascar, sir? Why?

Consalvo. Yellow fever is said to be raging there. I had hoped you might catch it. But I realized on reflection that your mere decease would solve nothing. Whatever may be the purpose of the infantile lies invented by that young woman and confirmed by yourself, the one clear fact is that you have publicly disgraced the good name of my sister and myself. I consider it essential on behalf of my sister and myself that you should repair the damage you have done. And repair it you shall. Mr Moesse, you will kindly demand of me in the warmest manner you can command, the hand of my sister in . . .

Noemi (*in a low voice*) No, Consalvo. I've given him up.

Consalvo. What? What do you mean?

Noemi. I want no more to do with him.

Consalvo (*outraged*) You mean you're throwing the whole thing up?

Noemi. Yes.

Consalvo (*moving to* R *of Noemi; aghast and trying to coax her*) But, Noemi, my dear: you've been hammering it into my head for days: you've compelled me to fabricate things which might have come from some cheap novelette; you've made me traipse hundreds of miles under blazing sun and pouring rain. And after all that, you say you're going to give him up. All this tarradiddle about duty and fatal consequences and I don't know what, is just a tale they've made up to deceive us: surely you must see that? This young man has simply told a lie. (*He moves menacingly to Alberto*)

Ofelia. Yes. I said so! Alberto couldn't!

Alberto (*indignantly*) Of course I could!

(Ofelia, *overcome by horror, wails and retires* L)

Noemi (*in a low voice*) It was his telling the lie that made me realize—that I've never meant anything to him. (*She weeps*)

Francesca (*suddenly*) Ah, no. Don't cry, Noemi. Don't cry, my dear, don't cry. (*She crosses to Noemi*)

(Noemi *puts her hand on Francesca's shoulder and continues to weep.* Francesca *gently strokes her.* Consalvo *moves and hovers behind Noemi and Francesca*)

Consalvo. Come, come, Noemi.

Noemi. I want to go away. Take me away.

Consalvo. Of course, my dear.

NOEMI. I want to go home.

CONSALVO. Yes, my dear. We'll go. We'll go back home. Come.

FRANCESCA. Don't cry, Noemi. He isn't worth it. No man's worth a woman crying over him.

(NOEMI, *supported by* FRANCESCA, *and still in tears, moves to the doorway* L. *The unfortunate* ALBERTO *stands in disgrace behind the table*)

ALBERTO (*as the others reach the door; stammering*) I—I only wanted to say that—in view of the—the disclosure, I mean—I am prepared to—marry her.

CLEOFE (*like a pistol-shot*) Which?

ALBERTO (*frightened*) Why—F-Francesca.

FRANCESCA (*turning at the doorway; scornfully*) Disclosure! (*Solemnly*) Allow me to tell *you*, Alberto Moesse, that I wouldn't marry you, now, not even if they fetched the police and ordered me to. Come, Noemi, darling, let's leave him.

(NOEMI, FRANCESCA *and* CONSALVO *exit* L. *There is a pause.* CLEOFE *stands with her back to the fireplace.* OFELIA *subsides into the chair* L *of the fireplace. The outer door is heard opening and closing*)

ALBERTO (*indignantly*) I see. Did you hear that, Aunt Cleofe? Fine, isn't it? I give up a splendid career and a magnificent marriage. I run the risk of being sent to Madagascar and dying of yellow fever. I'm pushed over a cliff, I get soaked to the skin, I'm forced to hide in a stable, I allow myself to be described as a vile seducer: I, who could be pointed to as an example of virtue and chastity; and after all that—I find a girl saying to me—what did she say?

CLEOFE. That she wouldn't marry you even if they fetched the police. (*She sits on the settle*)

ALBERTO. Grateful, isn't it? Just so as not to contradict her; out of sheer delicacy, I let people believe I'm not only a seducer, and an illegitimate father, I let people defame me, slander me— and then—then . . . But do you know what I shall do? I'll marry the other. I'll marry Noemi. (*He moves towards the cow-shed door*) I'll just go and find my hat, and then I'll . . . (*He breaks off and turns towards the door down* L)

(FRANCESCA *enters hastily down* L)

FRANCESCA. Noemi left her scarf and mackintosh. Where . . .?

(CLEOFE *picks up the scarf and mackintosh, rises and holds them out*)

(*She crosses to the settle and takes the scarf and mackintosh*) Oh, thank you, Aunt Cleofe, I'll be back in a . . .

ALBERTO (*at once timid and brusque*) Francesca: you—you said you wouldn't marry me not even . . .

FRANCESCA. Not even if they fetched the police.

ALBERTO. I see; good. After all I've done for you. I'm glad to hear it. I know now what I must do, do you see? It wasn't because I was fond of you, see? I did it—just to help you, to make you happy. (*Wildly*) Were you, or were you not, in love with me?

FRANCESCA. I was, my dear. And now—a miracle's happened, Aunt Cleofe. I'm not, any longer. Do you know, all at once I realized, suddenly? It's all over. Like that. As if my sight had suddenly been restored.

ALBERTO. Your what?

FRANCESCA (*aggressively*) My sight. Restored. I can see you now as you are. And I don't want you any more.

CLEOFE (*vibrantly*) Good, Francesca. Splendid. You can always find people like him. You're cleverer than he is, and yet you loved him. He'd have made a victim of you.

FRANCESCA. I'm not such a fool as that.

CONSALVO (*off* L; *calling*) Miss Francesca!

FRANCESCA (*calling*) I'm just coming! (*To the others*) I really feel quite astounded to think I ever saw anything in him.

CLEOFE (*briskly*) Francesca: the doctor is waiting just down the road. In these things it's always best to follow one's instincts and strike while the iron is hot. Do you want me to tell him to come up here?

FRANCESCA. Yes, Aunt. Yes. Certainly.

CONSALVO (*off; calling*) Miss Francesca!

FRANCESCA (*handing the mackintosh and scarf to Cleofe*) Will you please give them these things, Aunt Cleofe, and say good-bye to them for me? And tell the doctor to come in here.

CLEOFE. Yes, my dear, of course I will. (*She crosses to the doorway down* L) Come, Miss Ofelia.

OFELIA (*rising*) Everything seems to be going round and round. (*She moves to the doorway down* L)

CLEOFE (*briskly*) No, it doesn't. Come.

(OFELIA *and* CLEOFE *exit down* L)

ALBERTO (*moving to* R *of the table; angrily*) What utter nonsense! I suppose you think you can make me angry? Some hopes. How stupid. Sight restored, indeed! I never heard such nonsense.

FRANCESCA (*moving to the fireplace and picking up her jacket*) Yes, Alberto. You went on too long, seeing nothing.

ALBERTO. Yes, because I've no brains, because I'm backward.

FRANCESCA (*putting on her jacket*) No: I was used to that. I'd accepted it. It was when you admitted you'd had your way with me—with "fatal consequences". You poor creature!

ALBERTO (*furiously*) But I only said that so that they wouldn't find you out in a lie. Did you say it, or didn't you?

FRANCESCA. Yes, but you let them believe it. You were delighted. You went too far.

ALBERTO. *Me!*

FRANCESCA. Yes. And I suddenly felt such contempt for you, such loathing . . .

ALBERTO. Oh! So you loathe me now, do you? Let me tell you . . .

FRANCESCA (*moving slowly to* R *of the settle*) Alberto: when I look back on all the things I've done for you, all these years, but especially today, I shudder at the thought of it.

(*The* DOCTOR *enters* L *and comes a couple of paces into the room*)

Good evening, Doctor.

(*The* DOCTOR *has evidently prepared a difficult speech, which he is bent on delivering*)

DOCTOR. Good evening. Your respected aunt, who has for many years now honoured me . . .

ALBERTO (*moving to Francesca*) The things you've done for me? What do you . . .?

FRANCESCA. Yes, it was all your fault. You roused awful criminal instincts in me, from deep down.

ALBERTO. Doctor: I'm a criminal influence now!

DOCTOR. Your respected aunt, whose continued confidence in me . . .

FRANCESCA (*ignoring him*) Yes, all those lies and impostures: they were all your fault!

DOCTOR. Your respected aunt . . .

FRANCESCA. You forced me to make up the most disgusting tales, and deceive decent and well-meaning people; you made me push you off the mountain.

ALBERTO (*ferociously*) And I suppose all these scratches on my face are my fault, eh?

FRANCESCA. Yes. And you made me make up nasty, rude stories and be a laughing stock to everyone, as if I were another Noemi, half-dressed in a hut for cement and hydraulic lime.

ALBERTO. Doctor, she says it was me!

DOCTOR. The reason I am persuaded to present myself here . . .

ALBERTO (*ignoring him*) It's my fault if it rains, I suppose? If the cows' milk goes wrong tomorrow, it's all because of me.

FRANCESCA. Of course it is. You made me ashamed of myself. And now it's over, you understand? Even if I did once feel a little fond of you, it's all over and done with now. Ah, Doctor, if you only knew how happy I feel! Let's go, Doctor, I seem to be breathing fresh air for the first time for years.

DOCTOR. The true reason for my visit here . . .

ALBERTO (*shouting*) All right, then, if you want to know, I used to be in love with *you*. Once. I never realized: but whenever I used to come back home, in the train, I was as happy as anything; I used to whistle so loudly that everyone used to turn round and look. A man once told me to stop. "Stop it", he said. And do you know why I was happy? It was because of you. Because I was going to see you so soon, and talk to you. A little while ago, when I came down the mountain to look for you, I got soaked to the skin, I might have fallen in a ditch and died, too. And I would never have complained. Why? Because it was all for you. I might have caught a chill—and perhaps I have caught one, too: listen. (*He forces a cough*) And it didn't matter, because I loved you. (*He moves towards the table*) And *now*, do you want to know? Exactly the same thing has happened to *me*. It's all over.

FRANCESCA. It is just as well.

ALBERTO. In the very moment when I realized that I'd always loved you, ever since I was a boy, in that very same moment, *bonk*! It was all over.

DOCTOR. It is precisely for that reason, Miss Francesca, that your aunt, who . . .

ALBERTO (*shouting*) You've told too many lies! I can't bear people who tell lies. This is the end. It's all over. And better for everyone.

FRANCESCA. Certainly it's better for everyone. Good night. (*She crosses to the Doctor*) Doctor, you were quite right to come.

ALBERTO (*beside himself*) I'll marry Noemi. I've made up my mind. I'll go and get my hat, and then I'll marry her. She really loves me.

(ALBERTO *exits to the cow-shed*)

DOCTOR. Miss Francesca, your respected aunt, who has for many years honoured me with her trust, has been so kind as to advise me that I now might, or rather must, or—to put it more accurately perhaps—that the moment has now arrived when . . .

(ALBERTO *enters from the cow-shed. He carries a battered hat*)

ALBERTO (*furiously*) Look at it! Look at my hat. The cows have been trampling all over it. Even my hat's ruined! Never mind, though!

FRANCESCA (*close to the Doctor*) It's useless running after Noemi. She has already told you . . .

ALBERTO (*disgusted*) That she won't have me either, yes! First you all want me, then none of you want me. The sincerity of it. Never mind, I'll go my own way, I don't care a damn for any of you. Do you see what the result is? I've caught a cold. (*He makes himself cough*) I knew it. I can feel a tickling in my throat, it's always the sign. Good-bye.

FRANCESCA. Good-bye.

ALBERTO (*furiously*) And if you want to know, I don't want either of you: neither you nor her. You don't deserve me. You don't understand me. Even with you, I should always have been wasted. You're a little hypocrite. A snake in the grass.

FRANCESCA. And you're a liar.

ALBERTO (*shouting*) I like sincere, genuine people who say what they mean. An old cabbage like the doctor, that's the sort of thing you deserve.

DOCTOR. Oh, please, I beg you . . .

FRANCESCA. You don't even make me angry; I just feel sorry for you.

DOCTOR. And I never touch cabbage, as it happens.

FRANCESCA. What do you expect of him, Doctor? He's just a bad lot.

DOCTOR (*scientifically*) Psychologically a—subnormal—the debile-unstable type——

ALBERTO. What?

DOCTOR. —with characteristics of turbulent immorality and antisocial egotism. The two often go together.

(ALBERTO *moves behind the settle, picks up a large broom and brandishes it*)

ALBERTO. Doctor: would you be so good as to explain what you think you're doing here?

DOCTOR. The young lady's aunt, whose complete trust in me sometimes surprises me. . . .

ALBERTO. There's nothing for you to do here. There's no-one ill here.

DOCTOR (*bitingly*) Who knows, who can tell? A good doctor is always useful.

ALBERTO. But if anything were to happen to *you* in here, we should need another doctor.

DOCTOR. Please, please. Come. Come, come, come. I am here in order to offer this young lady the disinterested support of a gentleman—who is, I may say—(*with a contemptuous glance at Alberto*) a real man, who has his head fixed on in the correct manner, the right way round.

ALBERTO (*moving to the Doctor*) Oh, you have, have you? Just explain what you mean by that.

DOCTOR (*with a pitying look at Alberto; solemnly*) I am here, Miss Francesca, to place my mackintosh round your shoulders, so that you do not get wet as you issue from these premises, and also that you may, from that simple gesture, divine what it means to have ever at your side a person whom not even the rain can take by surprise.

ALBERTO. But she can have *my* mackintosh!

FRANCESCA (*dignified*) No, Alberto. It is too late.

DOCTOR. You, sir, have already demonstrated your unsuitability. Allow me. (*He puts his mackintosh round Francesca's shoulders*)

FRANCESCA. Thank you, Doctor. (*She pauses. Sadly*) Alberto:

there comes a day in our lives when we wake up in the morning still a child—and by nightfall we have become grown-up. The time for games and day-dreaming is over.

(ALBERTO *moves sadly to the table*)

DOCTOR. And more durative affections supervene, calculated to be a stay and comfort in the inevitable rubs and misfortunes of later life.

FRANCESCA (*with tears in her voice*) Good-bye, Alberto. It used to be so lovely to hear your voice in the garden.

ALBERTO (*without looking at Francesca; huskily*) Do you remember, Francesca—those picnics together: such splendid jam. What appetites we had, how happy we were . . .

FRANCESCA (*much moved*) And now the garden will never again seem to me so beautiful or so green. The days will never again have such a bloom upon them.

ALBERTO (*almost crying*) What makes me sorrier than anything, oh, my poor Francesca, is the thought of leaving you there —(*with sincere desolation*) in the hands of that dreadful old quack.

FRANCESCA (*with melancholy resignation*) How should it be else, Alberto?

DOCTOR. I must say I find that remark rather questionably put!

ALBERTO. A man who will always rouse shivers of disgust in you.

DOCTOR. I would ask you kindly to note . . .

FRANCESCA. I shall try my best, Alberto.

ALBERTO. You will pass your days surrounded by the stink of carbolic acid and mortuary chambers. And my own life—will be no better. (*He moves away in the direction of the cow-shed, almost weeping*) Good-bye, Francesca.

FRANCESCA (*stopping him; tremulously*) Alberto. Where are you going now?

ALBERTO (*tragically*) Where should I go? I don't know.

FRANCESCA. Don't be silly. You can't go out like that without your hat. You're still soaking wet.

ALBERTO (*with melancholy indifference*) What should it matter to me any more?

(*The* FARMER *enters* R. *He carries a tray with a cup of coffee*)

FARMER. Young sir: here's your coffee: you're not going away without drinking it, are you? (*He puts the tray on the table*)

ALBERTO (*staggered*) *My* coffee?

FRANCESCA (*dropping her eyes*) Yes. I asked them to make some for you, Alberto. I saw how wet you were, and—(*suddenly energetic, she crosses to Alberto and almost drags him towards the fire*) can't you ever realize how delicate you are? You must look after yourself, or you really will catch cold, of course you will. Come here, come and drink this nice coffee. (*She moves to the table and picks up the cup*

of coffee) Sit down there, near the fire. The coffee will do you good.
(*She hands the coffee to Alberto*)

(*The* FARMER *exits to the cow-shed*)

ALBERTO (*sitting on the settle*) Oh, how *kind* you are, Francesca·
(*He begins to stir his coffee, looking triumphantly at the Doctor*)

(FRANCESCA *removes the mackintosh from her shoulders, crosses and
restores it to the Doctor*)

FRANCESCA (*with dignity*) I must return your mackintosh to
you, Doctor. Thank you. You are able to think of such things for
yourself. But Alberto isn't. He has to have someone to think of
them for him.

DOCTOR. But what of his outrageous conduct? What of that?

FRANCESCA. This is the only way I know to make him pay for
it. (*She points to Alberto*)

(ALBERTO *coughs*)

Doctor, is that cough serious, do you think?

DOCTOR. As a general rule, such coughs are of but little
moment. Nevertheless and unfortunately, one can occasionally
begin by having a slight cough—and that slight cough can quickly
lead to the grave. (*He raises his hat._Courteously*) And should that
happen in this case, Miss Francesca, if you would like me to—
then I will, all patiently, *wait.*

ALBERTO *bends down impetuously and picks up the fire-tongs from
the hearth. The* DOCTOR, *putting the worst construction on this gesture,
disappears rapidly in the direction of the outer door as—*

the CURTAIN *falls*

FURNITURE AND PROPERTY LIST

ACT I

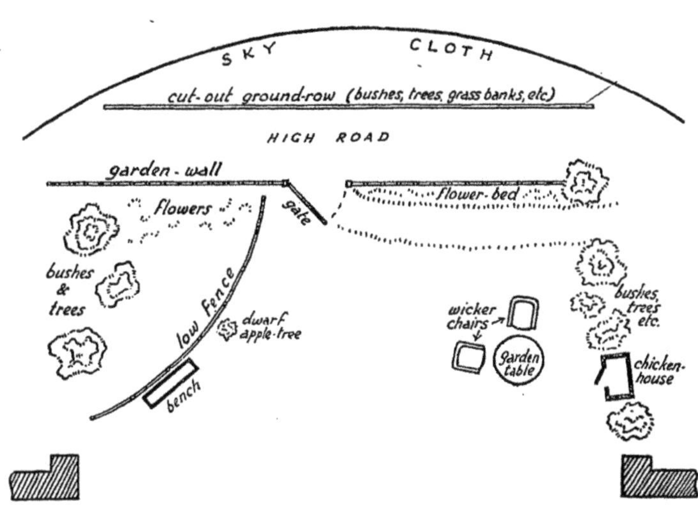

A Ground plan

On stage—Dwarf apple tree. *On it:* 5 apples
       Low bench (R)
       2 basket chairs. *On them:* cushions
       Table. *On it:* breadboard, French bread, bread knife, butter in dish,
           butter knife, salami, small sharp knife, large napkin

Off stage—Plate of tarts (ADELAIDE)
       Tray. *On it:* pot of coffee, cup and saucer (ADELAIDE)
       Car. *In it:* doctor's bag, doctor's raincoat, large umbrella, travelling
           rug (DOCTOR)
       Straw bag. *In it:* omelette in napkin, bottle of rum (ADELAIDE)
       Francesca's parasol (ADELAIDE)
       2 picnic baskets (ADELAIDE)
       Hammer (OFELIA)
       2 telegrams (POSTMAN)
       Marine binoculars (OFELIA)
       Motoring goggles (CLEOFE)
       Gladstone bag, walking-stick (CONSALVO)
       Umbrella (CLEOFE)

Personal—CLEOFE: spectacles
       COMMERCIAL TRAVELLER: fountain pen in box
       NOEMI: parasol

ACT II

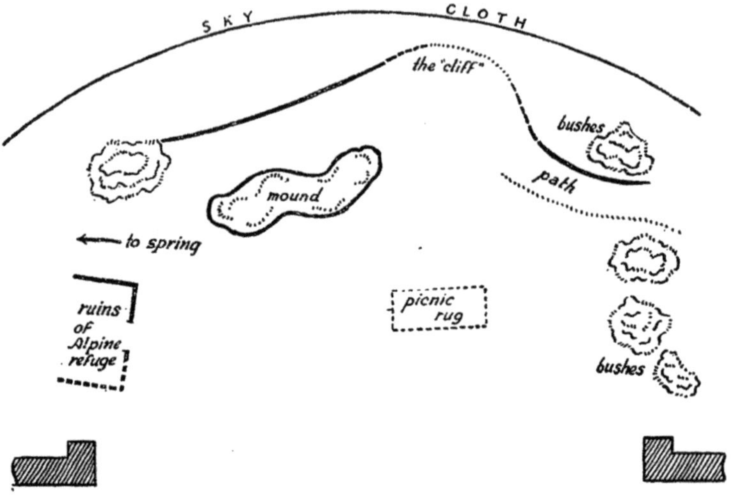

B Ground plan

Off stage—Picnic basket. *In it:* food, etc. (ALBERTO)
　　　　Straw bag. *In it:* bottle of rum, omelette in napkin (ALBERTO)
　　　　Travelling rug (ALBERTO)
　　　　Parasol (FRANCESCA)
　　　　Parasol (NOEMI)
　　　　Umbrella (DOCTOR)
　　　　Doctor's bag. *In it:* rolled crepe bandage, plaster, stethoscope,
　　　　　　　　bottles, etc. (DOCTOR)
　　　　Gladstone bag, walking-stick (CONSALVO)
　　　　Marine binoculars (OFELIA)

Personal—ALBERTO: watch, box of matches, packet of cigarettes
　　　　NOEMI: raincoat

ACT III

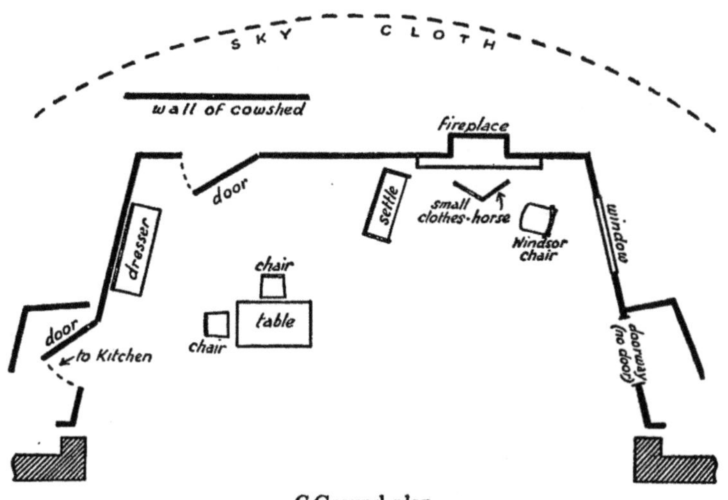

C Ground plan

On stage—Dresser
  Kitchen table. *On it:* cloth
  2 upright chairs
  Settle
  Windsor chair
  Large broom
  Clothes-horse. *On it:* Francesca's jacket
  Fire grate
  Fire-irons
  Window curtains
  Pendant light
  Light switch (above doorway L)

In cow-shed—Battered duplicate of Alberto's hat

Off stage—Francesca's parasol (ALBERTO)
  Gladstone bag, walking-stick (CONSALVO)
  Parasol (NOEMI)
  Large umbrella (CLEOFE)
  Binoculars (OFELIA)
  Tray. *On it:* large cup of coffee (FARMER)

Personal—NOEMI: handbag. *In it:* mirror

LIGHTING PLOT

Property Fittings Required: fire grate, pendant with shade

ACT I   Exterior. A cottage garden
     THE MAIN ACTING AREAS ARE—at a table LC, at a bench R, C and up C
To open: Effect of bright Summer morning sunshine
No cues

ACT II   Exterior. An Alpine spot
To open: Effect of bright Summer mid-day sunshine

Cue 1   At rise of CURTAIN   (page 22)
           Commence slow dim of light as the storm clouds gather

Cue 2   NOEMI: "Good afternoon"   (page 31)
           Commence slow raise of lights as the storm passes

Cue 3   ALBERTO: ". . . much of that rum?"   (page 40)
           Commence sunset effect

Cue 4   DOCTOR: "Look up. Quietly"   (page 42)
           Commence dim of lights as night begins to fall

ACT III   Interior. A farmhouse room. Night
     THE APPARENT SOURCES OF LIGHT ARE—a shaded pendant C and a fire
     up L
To open: The stage in darkness
           Dark outside window
           Fire lit

Cue 5   The FARMER switches on light   (page 45)
           Snap in pendant
           Snap in on-stage lights

www.ingramcontent.com/pod-product-compliance
Ingram Content Group UK Ltd.
Pitfield, Milton Keynes, MK11 3LW, UK
UKHW021822150726
7214IPUK00017B/275